Praise for SPY DAUGHTER, QUEER GIRL

"The fierceness of Absher's courageous quest to learn the gut-wrenching truths of her father's obfuscations parallels her search for her own truths in struggling to know herself as a gay woman ... This book is a treasure."
–Kathryn Watterson, author of *Women in Prison, Not by the Sword,* and *I Hear My People Singing*

"A riveting examination of identity and how the people who raise us make us—and how we all must continually remake ourselves. A moving portrait of a father-daughter relationship defined by secrets so big they spanned continents. Absher writes with heart, humor, and the grace that comes with forgiveness—the ultimate mission impossible."
–Jessica Pearce Rotondi, author of *What We Inherit: A Secret War and a Family's Search for Answers*

"Leslie tells her story with soul-searing honesty, plenty of self-deprecation and humour. In working through her own story, confronting her difficult past, she's revealed the human damage—most often to innocents—inflicted by the espionage 'game' played out on the global chessboard."
–Ian Callaghan, producer of the Audible Original series *My Dad the Spy*

"A gut-wrenching portrait of a daughter in search of her father's love, affection and attention, with Greece as a backdrop and the CIA always in the shadows. It is a cautionary tale about the effects of parental neglect, and ultimately a long overdue and touching reconciliation between father and daughter. I loved the book as a Greek American, a former CIA officer, and the father of a brave LGBTQ activist who may have felt many similar emotions growing up in a CIA family."
–Marc Polymeropoulos, former CIA senior intelligence officer & author of *Clarity in Crisis: Leadership Lessons from the CIA*

"In rich crisp prose, Leslie Absher immerses the reader into a world of espionage, loss, love, and becoming. With a literary deftness for observations, Absher is able to depict her early life with a tangible vividness that creates a symbiotic relationship between author and reader that elevates the book beyond a simple retelling of an interesting life."

–Kacy Tellessen, author of *Freaks of a Feather: A Marine Grunt's Memoir*

"As the child of intelligence officers, I was deeply moved by Leslie Absher's book. More than a poignant memoir, it is a thrilling detective story where the stakes are both unique to the child of an intelligence officer and painfully universal. It is a beautiful and expertly crafted exploration of our need for love, connection, and home. Her story broke my heart and engrossed me the whole way."

–Sophia Glock, cartoonist and author of the graphic memoir *Passport*

"Without a drop of sentimentality but with a giant heart and a fresh, assured voice, Absher explores the roles of memory, secrets, and the grief that comes from what we hide and what we leave behind—and what we simply cannot."

–Natalie Bakopoulos, author of *Scorpionfish* and *The Green Shore*

"*Spy Daughter, Queer Girl* is a family saga, a coming-of-age and a coming-out story, an inside view of CIA operations in Greece and other countries, and a mystery. With prose as bright and clear as an alpine lake, Absher lays bare the complexities of her own story side-by-side with her quest to understand her father. Spoiler alert: the jewel at the heart of the labyrinth is love."

–Alison Luterman, poet, essayist, and author of *Feral City* and *In the Time of Great Fires*

SPY DAUGHTER
QUEER GIRL

A MEMOIR

IN SEARCH OF TRUTH AND ACCEPTANCE

IN A FAMILY OF SECRETS

LESLIE ABSHER

Spy Daughter, Queer Girl
In Search of Truth and Acceptance in a Family of Secrets

Copyright © 2022 Leslie Absher

Book and cover design by Kevin Breen

ISBN: 978-1-957607-03-0
Cataloging-in-Publication Data is available upon request

Manufactured in the United States of America

Published by
Latah Books, Spokane, Washington
www.latahbooks.com

Latah Books and the author are grateful to Spokane Arts for its generous support of this
project.

To my wife, Susan, who has witnessed so many of my seasons and whose courage I used as my own until I was ready. And to the voice within, the one that always knew what was possible, and always led me to myself.

Prologue

I didn't know what the visit would be like. We hadn't seen each other since I moved to California four years earlier. At 67, Dad was still going strong—teaching and consulting—but I wondered if we would ever feel close. We knew so little about one another. Could this visit change any of that? Should I even go? As the day of my flight approached, it became too late to back out. I flew to Texas, rented a car and drove to the restaurant where we had agreed to meet. The heat hit me like an oven blast as I climbed out of the car. *You can do this*, I said to myself.

It was midday and quiet when I stepped inside. A handful of customers sat at tables beside a bank of windows. I saw my father up ahead. As he talked with the hostess, she kept her focus on him, nodding and grabbing menus without breaking eye contact.

"Hi, Dad," I said, coming up from behind.

He turned and smiled.

The bulky fabric of his navy blue suit jacket bunched under my arms as I reached up for a hug. He looked the same as last time—tall, medium build, hair completely white.

We followed the hostess toward the back, passing tables cleared from lunch but not yet reset, and arrived at a booth. I slid in and opened the oversized menu but couldn't concentrate.

"You hungry?" he asked.

"A little," I said.

The waitress brought water and a basket of tortilla chips, and we ordered enchiladas. Dad turned to the TV over the bar where a football game played with the sound turned down. I had the feeling that the visit was already slipping away. *I shouldn't have come*, I thought. This was how all of our visits ended up. I started to shrink into myself.

"Is there anything you want to know?" Dad said, jolting me from my retreat.

I grabbed the straw from my water glass, pulled it into my lap, and started twisting it between my hands. "Have you ever killed anyone?"

If Dad was taken aback by my bluntness, he didn't show it. But then he never did. He tended to stay cool while I sweated it out.

"I've made decisions that resulted in the loss of life," he said. Behind the thick-lensed glasses, his small, light blue eyes slipped into shadow.

I tried to work out what he meant by this. Had he ordered people killed? Passed along information that resulted in someone being assassinated? At thirty-seven, I only knew the bare minimum about his missions—that he started out working on the Cuban Missile Crisis, got transferred to Greece and after that, Vietnam. Vietnam. Maybe that's where he made decisions that "resulted in the loss of life," as he put it. Or did that happen in Greece? I reminded myself that this was what happened in wars, both overt and covert. People got killed. Still, I was shocked. He wasn't some nameless, faceless spy. He was Dad. My dad. His answer sounded evasive and cagey, and I wanted something real.

But bringing up what I especially wanted to know—if he had helped set up the 1967 Greek coup—felt dangerous, riskier even than asking if he'd ever killed anyone. We didn't have a great track record for talking about anything personal—not about his secrets, or mine, or our family's.

"What about Greece?" I asked.

Dad's hand stopped on its way back from the tortilla basket, a couple of chips clutched between his fingers. "What about it?"

"What was the CIA doing there?"

"We were fighting the communists."

"But didn't we help the Greek military pull off a coup which led to a dictatorship?"

"We had no idea about that. We were focused on other things."

He was making it sound like the Greek military and the CIA never crossed paths. As if "the colonels," as the dictators came to be called, had arrested and tortured people in some other Greece, not the Greece where we had lived and where he had worked.

"I've heard horrible stories," I said, recalling what friends had told me—instances of guns shoved into faces, people dragged from their homes and beaten inside dark cells. My voice wobbled. I pushed the sharp edge of the creased straw deeper into my palm, wishing I had some kind of proof or at least more information.

"Were your friends on the ground?" Dad popped the chips into his mouth, brushed his fingers together to dust off the salt, and reached for his water glass.

I watched a single ice cube slide into his mouth. I had no idea what he meant by "on the ground." Was he talking about troops, soldiers on a battlefield? The people who told me stories of torture were friends I had met in my twenties after college—not soldiers, just citizens.

"Yes," I said.

"Well, so was I, and there was none of that."

Dad lowered his water glass. Subject closed. Conversation over. This was what always happened. I sounded lame, and he sounded right.

When the food arrived, Dad hunched over his plate to eat. Every now and then, he looked over at the television, which was now a shiny black surface. I had other questions, but what was the point? It was 2002, and even though Dad had been retired for over ten years, it didn't matter. He'd never tell me the truth. Besides, if

I kept pushing for answers, I might lose the tiny, anemic shard of a relationship we had. *Barely* had. And for what? What did I think this would help me understand anyway? I finished my cheesy enchiladas and watched Dad pay the check in silence.

I didn't know it then, but my search for answers about my father and our secret CIA life was just beginning. One day, I thought I might write about his role, the CIA's role in the Greek coup. A journalist's investigation into history, full of dates and facts. At least that's what I thought it would be about—an exposé of his guilt, his culpability. I couldn't anticipate the ways it would evolve into a story about secrets. My father's *and* mine. And that in the end, it wouldn't only be about secrets; it would be about love too.

For issues of privacy, many of the names in the following text have been changed, especially anyone associated with the agency.

DAUGHTER

1. Greece, 1966

My memories of childhood begin in Athens. I have a handful of vivid recollections. Stitched together, they tell the story of a child who felt safe and loved. Sometimes, I wonder what happened in between these vignettes. What have I forgotten and why? Memory is fallible. Unreliable. The only story I can really tell is the one held by my heart. The one I feel in my bones.

I was a baby when we moved into a modest-sized house in Old Psychiko, the neighborhood of embassies and mansions. It was a comfortable home, but as soon as I could walk, I left it for the yard. I spent entire afternoons chasing our scrawny cat through the rose garden and watching goldfish dart through the shadows of our pond. When I grew tired, I sat under the fig tree and listened to the wind rustle its leaves. Leaves as rough as sandpaper, as wide as a giant's hand.

A year after we arrived, my sister was born. Mama lifted her out of the hospital basinet, where a nurse had pinned a tiny blue evil eye to keep her safe and brought her home. Evelyn was wrapped in a white blanket like all Greek babies, but her bald head and pink skin showed a lighter complexion. I held her soft living body in my arms. My world expanded just then. Before, I had my yard and Anna, my nanny. Now I had a sister.

But for others, life was perilous.

Ten days after Evelyn was born, the Greek military rolled its tanks into the city center and took over the government. The world's oldest democracy turned into a dictatorship overnight. A group of colonels—not generals as some had predicted—began arresting anyone who spoke out. They were sent to remote islands for years. Famous artists and composers were arrested and sent away too. The press was censored. I didn't know any of this then. I had no idea what took place down the avenues inside interrogation centers like the one on Bouboulinas Street. I was happy in my garden.

***

On Sundays, we piled into the family car and drove to a nearby taverna. Outdoor tables listed atop uneven ground and stereo speakers sat high in the plane trees, tied to leafy branches like overgrown crows. The waiter spread paper across the surface of the table and clipped it to the sides so the wind would not take it. He pulled a pad of paper from his pocket, a pencil from behind his ear, and wrote our order in the book—lamb chops, a village salad, and mustard greens.

The food arrived on large, family-style plates. Mama cut the meat into small pieces for me and Evelyn, while Dad pushed bread into the green olive oil at the bottom of the salad bowl. I loved pulling food from the generous serving dishes. At home, we ate like Americans, everyone with their own dish. But at a taverna, we ate the Greek way. Greeks didn't wait or ask permission; instead, they just had at it. I stabbed at the oily greens called *horta* and let forkfuls melt inside my mouth.

When there was nothing left but crumbs, we said, "*Hortasame.*" We're stuffed. Mama and Dad lit cigarettes and sat back, full and happy, as the four of us listened to bright, jangling *bouzouki* music play from the speakers overhead. I felt safe inside moments like these. Happy. It was a feeling that would stay with me my whole life.

***

Another snapshot comes to mind—the days our yard was filled with fancy people, men in crisp shirts and women in bright evening dresses. They talked and laughed and milled around the fishpond. I carried a small tray from one group to another, offering *mezedes*, Greek appetizers. Everyone smiled and greeted me, but I hated my cramped patent leather shoes and having to talk to strangers. When Mama, tall and pretty in her sleeveless dress and tan espadrilles, wasn't looking, I grabbed Evelyn's hand and led her along the edge of the party to the grape arbor. We dropped cross-legged onto the dirt and peered out from under the canopy of leaves. It felt good to hide inside this secret world. A tight green coil of mosquito repellent sat in the corner. Black smoke spewing from its burning head entranced me. The pungent odor stung my eyes, but I didn't mind. It was the smell of summer, the smell of my yard.

There were other outdoor nooks that I loved too, places I sat with Mama and Evelyn in the afternoons, when she led us to the stone bench in the backyard. After giving us a hug, we settled in for storytelling. "Be very quiet. We don't want the fairies to hear us. They don't like loud noises," she whispered.

I stayed perfectly still.

"Thumbelina's flying to a fairy gathering on her beautiful monarch butterfly," Mama said, arching her dark brows.

The idea of riding a butterfly captivated me.

"What does Thumbelina look like?" I whispered, wondering if she had brown hair like me.

Mama answered, "She has wispy blond hair and silver wings." Mama raised her finger to her red lipstick lips. "Y'all hear that?"

We squinted into the pine trees.

"Those are fairy tambourines," she said.

I quieted my breath until I could hear the faint sounds of the delicate orchestra filtering down from the high up branches. I sensed magic everywhere, the possibility of things.

***

I loved being with Mama, but I loved Anna too.

Anna was nineteen when she left her village to come to Athens and take care of me and my sister. She had short light brown hair, kind eyes and always wore dresses. She gave me a book of Greek nursery rhymes and helped me to read the simple sentences. One afternoon, in the garden, I managed to read a sentence on my own. I raced into the house and found Anna in her small basement room. She pulled me onto her lap and listened to me sound out the words. When I was done, she gave me a hug. I felt Greek then, just like Anna.

For Easter, Anna placed small bowls of red dye on the kitchen table, next to a basket of cold, hardboiled eggs. She invited me and Evelyn to choose one. I snatched the biggest and dropped it into the bowl. I wanted my egg to be as bright as the geraniums on our front porch, but I had no patience. When I lifted mine out too soon, it was a watery pink.

Evelyn's quiet blue eyes peered at the egg as if it were a living creature speaking directly to her. She waited and waited. At the right moment, she lifted it from the bowl, blew on it and placed the deep red orb onto the paper towel.

Next, Anna showed us how to grip our eggs and click them together for *tsougrisma*, the egg-knocking game. If our egg didn't break, we would have good luck all year. One! Two! Three! I tapped my egg against Anna's, and tiny white cracks appeared on mine. Anna laughed, and I felt lucky anyway.

While Anna taught me and Evelyn Greek traditions, Mama made sure we celebrated Easter the American way. She outfitted us in matching white dresses and sent us out into the yard, our baskets filled with finely cut green paper. I started with the cotoneaster bushes. I peered past their red berry clusters into the cool, protected place they made against the side of the house. Nothing. I looked back at Mama standing on the porch, fair-skinned, her dark brown hair held under a scarf. She waved and gave me her big lipstick smile. I wandered over to the fig tree. On the ground, I noticed a single, carefully placed leaf, and beneath one of its wide fingers, the curve of a perfect yellow egg. Another snapshot of memory. That egg. I placed it inside my green nest. I felt proud. There was nothing I couldn't do, no mystery I couldn't solve.

***

One hot afternoon, I decided not to go into the house for a snack. There was a dark stuffiness indoors that made me want to stay away. I felt freer in the garden. That day, when I grew hungry, I reached for the cotoneaster berries at the front of the house. I pulled down a handful and popped them into my mouth. They tasted dry and only slightly sweet.

I told Evelyn what I had done. I'm not sure she felt the same way about being in the house, but she was my little sister and she always followed my lead. I watched as she grabbed a handful and pushed them into her mouth.

Once we started, we couldn't stop. It was not hunger. It was the velvety feeling of being sneaky.

I grew bolder after that. There were things I could do on my own, adventures I could have that Mama and Anna didn't need to know about. Standing beside the front gate one afternoon, a voice inside me whispered, *See what is outside the yard.* I pushed open the metal door. It felt scary to do this, but there was something on the other side of my fear that urged me to keep going. Something exciting and rewarding.

Evelyn stayed put. "Don't," she begged.

I ignored her and stepped onto the noonday sidewalk. Old Psychiko was quiet. There were no stores, no kiosks, no *kafenions* with old men drinking small cups of espresso, just houses and embassies shaded by plane trees. I was five years old and had never been outside the yard on my own. The day suddenly felt fresh. I liked this feeling, the world expanding before me.

This is easy, I thought to myself. *There is no danger here.*

Then I noticed a man. He had dark hair and chin stubble and stood a few feet from our front gate.

"*Ela koritsi*," he called with a smile. Come here, girl.

People beckoned to me in this way every day. With my brown hair and eyes, I looked like a Greek girl. "*Ela!*" they said. Come! But I did not know this man.

"*Ela!*" he repeated.

Evelyn's fear pressed into my back.

There was something about his urgency I didn't trust. I took a step toward the gate, and when I did, the man frowned. His face twisted in anger. He cursed as I slipped inside the safety of the yard. My hands gripped the iron bars as I watched him turn and walk away.

I told no one about this stranger. Was he targeting Dad or our family? Trying to kidnap me? Perhaps he was simply a man who preyed on children. I folded this memory into the back of my mind and told no one. Not Mama and not Anna. I had grown accustomed to the natural weight of deception by then.

***

Another image, vivid and enduring—a scorching hot day. Dad and I were at the beach. He held my hand as we waded into the sea. When it grew too deep for me to stand, I climbed onto his back and held tight. I breathed in the coconut smell of his neck. Like a starfish, I clutched his shoulders. I let him take the brunt of each wave onto his pale and hairless chest as we rode the waves. I felt only the gentle rise and fall of the swells. No sudden crashing or dose of water up my nose or down my throat. The sea was a harmless thing. I laughed at each dissipating crest. But when a big wall of water rose up, I ducked quickly behind his shoulders. I knew everything would be okay and that he would always shield me.

2. San Antonio, 1971

I was six when we left Greece for Texas. The walls of our new townhouse were thin, the rooms small. There was no fishpond, no juicy figs to make my mouth sticky and sweet. Our yard was full of crabgrass that itched my feet, and instead of open-air markets, we bought food from air-conditioned supermarkets. I didn't have a say in leaving Greece. If I had, I would never have agreed to go. I remember my father driving through the streets of Athens to the house belonging to the family that would be taking care of our dog. I remember confusion. Why were we leaving? Then we were in Texas. I had nightmares for weeks after we arrived—our house in Old Psychiko was on fire. Smoke engulfed the grape arbor. I searched for our cat. Where was Anna? I awoke terrified and crying. Mama and Dad came into the room Evelyn and I shared. They tried to comfort me but there was nothing they could do.

In Texas, I started to steal. I opened packages of cookies while standing inside empty store aisles. I ate a row and then shoved the box back onto the shelf. One day, I decided to go to the bakery. I smiled at the man behind the counter and asked if I could have a single glazed donut. He grabbed silver tongs and lifted a donut from a newly baked row. He placed it inside a wax bag and sealed it with a sticker. Inside a nearby aisle, I ripped open the bag and took a bite. It was gooey and wonderful. When I was finished, I balled up the bag and stuck it behind a row of cans. Stealing was easy. No one suspected a polite, smiling little girl. I did it a lot. I snuck food at home too. Mid-afternoons, I went into the kitchen, slid a short stack of white bread from the bag on the counter and left for the yard. Warmth emanated from the red bricks as I leaned against the side of the house and let the soft substance melt onto my tongue.

The only good thing about San Antonio was the pool. It was blue and wide and sat in the middle of our townhouse complex. One day, Dad stood in the shallow end in navy blue swim trunks. He explained how to swim to the end and back in one breath. His dark sunglasses stood out against his pale skin and sandy brown hair. He pumped air in and out of his lungs—puff, puff, puff. It looked like he was gulping it.

"Empty your lungs completely, then take one deep breath."

I watched as he pushed out all the air, stuck out his chest, and then dropped below the surface of the water. He shoved off from the wall and moved away from me like a blurry fish. When he reached the end, I saw him return and slowly come into view.

He popped up beside me. "You try it."

I pulled my goggles over my eyes, emptied my lungs, took in one giant breath, and dropped into the water. I swam just above the bottom, passing a waterlogged worm and a horseshoe-shaped nose plug. I reached the end, turned, and pushed off. Halfway back, I felt starved for air. *Almost there*, I told myself. I saw Dad's long legs as I approached the wall. My fingers felt the rough concrete before my head broke the surface. I yanked off my goggles, panting hard. Dad's trick had worked.

"You did it!" he said, smiling.

***

Swimming made me feel good, but stealing was a thrill. While Mama loaded her groceries onto the conveyor belt at the store one day, I noticed the yellow Juicy Fruit gum display. I grabbed a pack, opened it, and shoved two sticks into my mouth. The sugary flavor flooded me. I crammed in another two sticks. That's when Mama turned to see me.

She grabbed my chin. "Where did you get that gum?"

Terror pricked me. "I found it in your purse," I lied.

She narrowed her dark eyes but released my chin.

The next day I was in the kitchen, my skin tan and my hair still wet from the pool. Dad strode in. He was still in work clothes— dark slacks and a white short-sleeve dress shirt.

"Is there something you want to tell me?" he asked, leaning against the counter.

The gum. Mama told him. I knew it.

"No," I said, keeping my eyes on the floor.

"I want you to know you can always talk to me."

Maybe I can trust him, I thought. I wanted to. But this wasn't like him. He didn't often stop moving long enough to have conversations.

"I took some gum without paying for it," I said. The words seemed to scratch at my throat.

Dad's eyes stayed soft. "Was that the only thing you've stolen?"

I thought back on all the things I'd taken: cookies, glazed donuts, chocolate bars, Twizzlers. Taking things—*stealing*—made me feel alive again. The way I had felt every single day in Greece. I was sure that if I told him about all of it, I'd be in big trouble. I sensed his anger on a daily basis, just below the surface, even if he seldom let it boil over. *He's not angry*, the voice whispered. *Trust him.*

"I've taken candy too," I said. My heart pounded. I told him about each and every item I had stolen. All the unpaid bakery goods, the cookie packages I carefully opened, sampled, and then shoved back onto the shelf. With each confession, the tightness inside my throat eased.

"I'm glad you told me. I want you to promise you'll stop taking things without paying for them."

"I'll stop," I said, and I did. I couldn't explain to him then why I did it, that I was trying to replace the home I had lost. Still, telling helped.

***

Not long after our heart-to-heart, Dad announced that he was going to Vietnam. I'd seen demonstrations against the war in Vietnam on the news but knew little else about it. He told us he'd be gone for two years but that he'd be back to visit. He didn't say why he was going or what he would do there. When it came to his job, he never explained. The approachable Dad who had listened to my confessions of stealing was gone. In his place was a tighter, tenser father.

Then one afternoon, he left, and it was just me and Mama and Evelyn.

Both of my parents had grown up in San Antonio, so there was plenty of family around. We visited Mama's mother, Janet. She had thick white hair and dark eyebrows. When we hugged, my face pressed against her round belly held tight beneath a stiff girdle. Janet had a big backyard, but her next-door neighbor had a giant pecan tree. After getting permission, Evelyn and I collected pecans and brought them into Janet's yard. She gave us a hammer and a bowl. We cracked open shell after shell and placed the meat in the bowl.

Some days, Mama and Janet set up their easels in Janet's art studio and painted flower arrangements. On nice days, they took their paints to the river. When Mama got back home, she revealed to me and Evelyn what she had created. I loved the watery green-brown of the river and the way she depicted the graceful branches of the weeping willow.

Evelyn studied Mama's watercolors. She was a natural. When Mama brought out sketchbooks for us, we grabbed charcoals and drew the vase of flowers placed before us on the table. Evelyn moved her arm across the paper; her eyes fell into an art trance just like Mama's.

Then one day, something changed. Mama didn't talk as much as usual. She looked sad and left me and Evelyn with Janet. We started to visit Dad's parents more too. We went back and forth between grandparents with no explanation. Janet was the one who drove us to Grandmother and Grandfather's. Our two sets of grandparents were nothing like each other. Dad's parents were formal and proper, whereas Mama's were looser and more fun loving. Janet pulled up to the house and waved at Grandmother, but she wouldn't get out and say hello. She and Grandmother were never in the same room together, which made me wonder why.

Everything was okay until it wasn't.

This is the image I remember: I was six and Evelyn four and we were sitting on the sofa watching Mama pace the living room floor in her long flowing nightgown. Her bare feet pushed into the soft carpet. She said things that didn't make sense. What was she saying? Her tension penetrated me, but her words didn't. All I remember is fear and confusion. And knowing something was wrong. I felt the walls of our small home pressing in. Grownups weren't supposed to do irrational things like this. They were supposed to stay steady and predictable.

I came home from school the next day and found Mama missing. Grandmother was there instead. She said Mama had been taken to the hospital but didn't say why. Was she okay? I had many questions. Grandmother didn't answer them. Just like Dad, she didn't explain. Tall, dressed in a navy blue knee-length skirt, her hair tinted a light gold, she kept her face stony and closed.

Here is another recollection—when Mama went into the hospital, Dad came back from Vietnam. He stood on the sidewalk in front of our townhouse in a suit and wingtip shoes. His words were clipped. He said we had to live with Grandmother for a while. It was strange to see him standing before us when he had been gone for months. He was in a rush. He stayed a day or two, talked to Grandmother, and then drove to the airport and was gone again.

I wanted to know why we couldn't live with Janet. Who had decided where we would live? Dad? Grandmother? And what kind of sickness did Mama have? There was no information from the adults. Maybe there had been an explanation, something like, "Your mother needs help. The doctors said she should rest." All I remember is nothing. And the way my panicked questions seemed to irritate Grandmother. She was angry, and I was convinced it was my fault.

Our grandparents' house was quiet. Evelyn and I played "office" using stationery supplies from Grandfather's downtown Milam Building suite. In the afternoons, a kind Mexican woman named Maria came to clean and care for us. She pulled out ingredients from the kitchen cabinet and showed me how to make flour tortillas. "Push the roller until the dough is thin and round," she said. Sometimes, she took out small fabric squares and corn husks from a paper bag she had brought and showed us how to make dolls with cloth skirts and smiling faces.

On the weekends, Grandmother took us shopping for clothes. Instead of going to Sears like we did with Mom, Grandmother drove to a formal dress shop. Paisley print dresses, many with long sleeves, hung on circular racks. Grandmother pulled out a skirt and blouse set and held it up against my chest. I said I wanted jeans and striped T-shirts but I knew that wasn't what she had in mind. She frowned and said I needed something nice to wear. The saleswoman slipped a clear plastic sleeve over the skirt set and took Grandmother's credit card.

We went to see Mama a few times. Grandmother seemed tense as she drove, but I brimmed with excitement. We would finally see Mama! Grandmother stayed in the waiting room and sent me and Evelyn into the visiting area. Mama was there in her green hospital gown, her face pale with no makeup. I looked into her sad brown eyes and didn't know what to say.

Eventually, Mama recovered. After two months, she moved back home. We didn't talk about the hospital or why Mama had gone or how she felt now. Neither of my grandmothers brought it up. It would be years before we addressed it—me, Dad and Evelyn. By then, I would have my own ideas about what had happened and why. My anger solidified.

***

One day, I came across a bag of purple-green pistachios in the kitchen. I remembered eating them every time we went to the open-air market in Athens. I stood in the middle of the linoleum floor, cracking open shell after shell. It was the same salty tang from the market. The same soft meat. With each handful, I erased the distance between San Antonio and Athens. The pistachios seemed capable of giving me back my family. I ate and ate, hoping to make the taste of Greece and happiness last forever. I ate so many that I didn't notice my stomach filling, my throat thick, until it was too late. When my stomach rebelled, I ran to the bathroom to throw up. I didn't think it was possible to eat too many. My hunger for that part of my life was insatiable.

***

Eventually, Dad returned home from Vietnam. He brought arms full of gifts—dolls and record players and handcrafted textiles. We didn't talk about what he had done while he was away and why he had gone in the first place. Had it been worth it? Was the war won? I didn't know. We moved on as if it had been a blip—Dad leaving, Mama being hospitalized. We were a family in America again, and normalcy for us meant moving. We left San Antonio for Northern Virginia, and after two years there, we returned to Texas—Dallas this time. With each move, there was a new house, a new school. I felt numb. Every relocation, I had to start over and make new friends. My parents didn't get it. They acted like it should be easy, but it wasn't. At ten years old, I hated moving. Why did we always have to leave everything behind?

But I knew why.

One morning, I caught Dad as he crossed the off-white shag carpet of our tract home, heading toward the door—boxy briefcase in hand, suit jacket buttoned. He wasn't like other dads. I knew that by then. He looked over his shoulder, even when he was walking down wide, empty streets, and never invited neighbors over for backyard barbeques. If a neighbor said "Hi" in the morning, he gave a quick wave, but if they came over to talk, he cut things short.

He was almost at the door, about to reach for the knob, when I said, "Dad, what's your job?"

He turned around to find me standing before him wearing dark red Toughskin jeans—hands on my hips, my messy brown ponytail trailing my back.

He swept his light brown hair off his forehead and said, "I'm in the Army."

The tight feeling in the middle of my chest relaxed. I'd never seen him in a uniform, but I believed him. I wanted to. It made me proud to think of him as a soldier protecting America. Maybe this is what he was doing when he wasn't at home—protecting me and America.

But a month later, I heard Dad talking on the phone. "I'm with the State Department," he said to whoever was on the other end, his long frame bending over the table and his blue suit jacket falling open.

That chest tightening feeling returned. What happened to the Army?

I didn't want to think he was lying, but I wondered.

Maybe that's when the impulse to investigate him started, with that first lie. At ten years old, I suspected he wasn't who he said he was. My suspicion wasn't clear-eyed and focused.

It was fuzzy, muddled. When was he who he said he was, and when wasn't he? Most of the time, he seemed like a nerd. He said "Ma'am" and "Sir" and never cursed. Upright and clean cut. The most reliable person in the world. Until he said something that stuck in my mind, something I couldn't let go of. That's when I wondered if there was something wrong with me. Why couldn't I trust him, and who was he? I wanted to know the real Dad. The one beneath the shifting stories.

***

One afternoon, I was on my way out to ride my bike when my eye landed on one of his paperbacks with the word *Enemies* written on the spine. There was something about the word *enemies* that made me stop. I scanned his other books and saw that they were all about war.

I intercepted him when he came home from work. A voice said, *Don't bother him. You'll make him mad.* I did it anyway.

"Did you know that all of your books are about war?" I tried to steady the quaver in my voice. I knew what would happen next. He'd shake his head and tell me that he wasn't obsessed with war. But I'd be ready. I'd ask him to tell me the title of one non-war-related book. Just one. He wouldn't be able to, which would prove to him and to me that he wasn't like other fathers.

"You're right," he said calmly.

He acted as if he was the normal one. And maybe he was. Maybe it was me who wasn't.

"Don't you think that's a little strange?" I said, starting to sweat.

"Not at all."

I had hoped for more of an explanation. I wanted to ask, "Why are you so obsessed with war?" But I didn't ask this because I couldn't believe he thought being obsessed with war was okay. I stood mute until he turned on the heels of his black wingtips and disappeared into the den, leaving me with my unanswered question.

***

But there were other times too, when he was lighthearted, when we all were.

We would set up our TV trays in front of the set, eat pork chops and mashed potatoes, and watch *M*A*S*H*, the war comedy-drama series about a mobile army surgical hospital in South Korea during the Korean War. We laughed, Dad included, at the sharp-witted commentary by "Hawkeye" Pierce, played by Alan Alda. But the biggest laughs were always reserved for the character of Colonel Flagg with his absurd aliases and obvious disguises, the parody of a spy. In one episode, Flagg claimed to be a Chinese double agent while dressed like Benito Mussolini. Dad roared with laughter at that one. We all did.

Maybe shows like *M*A*S*H* were a release for Dad, a way to let go of his job, one in which he was obligated to think about war constantly. Shows let off steam, while other viewings reflected the seriousness he carried within him.

***

It was near midnight, and I had come downstairs for a glass of milk. Dad was in the living room in boxers and an undershirt, his eyes glued to the TV. Instead of going back upstairs, I hung around and started watching the movie. American soldiers slithered around on their bellies and dodged bullets fired from inside some jungle.

"What are they fighting about?" I asked.

As soon as I said this, Dad jumped up from his chair and disappeared into his office. A minute later, he was back, a piece of faded blue and red cloth in his hand. It looked like a rag.

"This is a Viet Cong flag. A communist flag. Communists want to take over the world! That's what the movie's about!"

His cheeks were shiny, and it felt like the war was in the room with us. He had gone to Vietnam. Did he fight the Vietcong? Is this why he was so worked up? And who was this dad anyway? This wasn't the composed father, the one always in control, who kept his feelings under wraps. This one was visibly worked up; he was almost yelling.

I stared at Mom's painting of daylilies hanging on the wood-paneled wall behind his head. It made him look like he was wearing a hat with bright orange flowers on it. I didn't get the word *communism* and how it connected to the movie he was watching, but Dad got it. He got it completely. It was an important word, a clue, and one he seemed to be entrusting to me. He stared at me. He needed me to understand. I nodded. I wanted him to know I was there for him. It was okay that he was all worked up. Dad took the flag back to the den.

When he returned, he was quieter. We watched the rest of the movie together in silence. I felt close to him, even though I didn't feel what he felt. At least he was showing me what went on in his mind. That's what mattered. But the next day, Dad came home from work and went straight into the den. He was back to his usual strained self. The moment we shared, the one where he showed this other side, the looser one, disappeared under the surface again, which is where my real family lived. Underneath.

***

Being told something real made me hungry for more. To know more, I realized I would have to sneak around and eavesdrop. It seemed like my only choice. So one afternoon, when the phone rang and Dad went to the bedroom to answer it, I dashed into the den and carefully picked up the receiver. I heard Mom's Texas drawl. She'd been gone from the house since morning.

"They found a lump," she said.

A lump? I'd heard about lumps. They were found in breasts, and they meant cancer, which was scary and horrifying and overwhelmed me. But I didn't say anything because I didn't want Mom to know I was listening in on her call with Dad. It felt dangerous to listen but irresistible too.

"I have to meet with a surgeon," she said.

My heart beat so loudly I couldn't concentrate, so I carefully lowered the receiver.

For the next few weeks, I worried. Would she be okay? Was she going to die?

An eternity passed until Mom sat me and Evelyn down at the table, her slender, pale arms crossed in front of her. "I have cancer and I'm going to have an operation," she said. "But after that, I'll be fine. Just fine."

Mom was calm and strong, but operations were bad news. I didn't want to think about what might happen if she wasn't fine. There were more things to worry about now. There was Dad's secret job and Mom's cancer. I stuffed my new worry below the surface.

Mom's operation went okay, in a way. Afterward, she sat at her dressing table in the mornings, like always, and applied dark green eye shadow and a light brushing of maroon powder onto her cheeks. Now, she slipped a rubbery yellow prosthesis into her bra. I tried not to stare at the empty place, dark and freckled, where her full breast used to be. She carefully changed the bandage under her arm, placing a clean one over the small opening in her skin.

"It won't close because of the radiation," she said when she caught me looking.

She rose, went over to the closet, and picked out a shirt. She used to wear sleeveless sundresses, but now she chose long-sleeved blouses.

After a few months, Mom's remission took hold. We didn't talk about disease. Ours wasn't a sick house. That had all washed away.

Still, cancer had left its mark. After she recovered, Mom's painting style changed.

Instead of sketching flowers at the kitchen table, she went to the garage, tucked her dark hair under a brightly patterned scarf, and unrolled a huge canvas on the cement floor. Usually she wore skirts, but that day she had put on jeans and a button-down shirt. She walked over to a gallon paint can, pried open the lid, and gracefully tipped it onto the rough cloth. A splash of sparkly copper paint rushed out. She did the same thing with another can and watched as a thick finger of silver ran across to meet the copper. Her cheeks flushed. She said she was making the paintings for a display window at Neiman Marcus. "I'll show you next week after they hang them up."

Mom wasn't the cautious mother she had been before. Now she was daring. Bold.

She enrolled in a clinical psychology program and bought books like The Feminine Mystique by Betty Friedan at a local bookstore. I snuck into her bedroom when she was out of the house and went through her drawers until I found *The Joy of Sex*. Graphic drawings of men and women in sexual positions shocked and then drew me in. My eyes slid across the woman's rounded hips and breasts, but the sight of the man's erect penis startled me. I stared at the different sexual positions and scanned the page, reading about *erections* and *intercourse*. Was that what I was supposed to do when I grew up? I closed the book and slipped it back into the drawer.

Each day on the bus to and from school, my best friend, Prisha, and I huddled in the back, passing notes. Our thighs touched as the bus rocked along. I tried to find the words to say how I felt for her.

"I'll never forget you," I wrote, "no matter what."

Prisha pressed the paper against her tanned thigh and wrote back to me. Her cursive looped across the paper, big and fat, "Don't let boys get between us EVER!!!"

I felt light and happy as I moved to the front of the bus. I grabbed the smooth chrome bar, ready to swing out into the Texas sunshine, when a boy by the door hissed, "Lezzie."

My joyful feeling fizzled. I stared straight ahead. I knew what *lezzie* meant, although I didn't know how I knew. It wasn't a good word. That's when it clicked. It was shameful to be who I was, to like girls. I felt stained by this word, exposed. Now, everyone would see who I was. *Hide who you are*, a voice inside warned, and so I did, even though I didn't fully know what I was hiding.

I see the impact of this incident now. The way it sent my feelings for girls underground and made me censor myself. I reasoned that as long as I didn't act too bold, I could hold onto my desire, and it would all work out. Did I reason this or was it subconscious? Either way, it had seemed like a reasonable strategy. *It's what our family did*, I thought as I made my way across the field of weeds toward our subdivision.

Not long after, I overheard Mom and Dad talking in hushed tones in the living room. I was upstairs in the hallway. I couldn't catch it all, but when I heard Mom say the word divorce, I dropped cross-legged onto the carpet to listen. The nubby threads itched my bare calves.

"What will you do for work?" Dad asked. I heard the words he didn't say: *What if you get sick again?*

"I'll find something," Mom said.

"What about the girls?"

I felt caught under a spotlight, like Mom and Dad could see me suspended above them.

"They'll come with me," Mom said.

Just when I thought they'd start to fight, they stopped talking. I got up quietly and went to my room. The whole next day, all I could think was that we might be leaving the brown, cracked dirt of Texas, which was the best possible idea. I couldn't wait to ditch boring jumbo supermarkets and new houses that all looked the same. We would stop going to Mom's Catholic Church on Sunday too. We never talked about the sermons later anyway. Or went to Dad's Episcopalian church. When he came to ours, he stood at the end of the row and looked uncomfortable. I wanted to leave all of that behind. Church. Boring Texas. We were off on an adventure, just Mom, Evelyn, and me. We would take Skylos too, who we gave the unimaginative name of "dog" in Greek. Maybe that's where we would go, some place exciting like Greece. I wanted to go back someday. And maybe that day was now because Mom wanted a divorce. Something about it seemed right. She was tired of all the moving too, tired of Dad's job controlling our lives. Even if we didn't go back to Greece, we could still pack the car and go somewhere, and I could escape my life. But weeks and months passed, and nothing happened. No divorce and no more conversations about leaving. Everything stayed exactly the same.

3. Abracadabra

For my twelfth birthday party, Dad set up his black lacquered magic stand in the living room and proclaimed in his usual baritone, "Welcome to Mike's Magic Show!" My friends were there, sitting on the carpet in front of him, waiting for things to disappear.

Dad took out a golf ball and placed it inside his left hand. He made a fist and moved his right hand over it, back and forth in a handwashing motion. He pivoted left and then right. He picked up his wand, waved it, and said, "Abracadabra." He opened his fist in a slow, dramatic way. It was empty. He did the same thing with the other hand, waved his wand, and miraculously the ball reappeared. All my friends were amazed, including Prisha, who smiled at me.

Dad moved on to his other tricks. He pulled a giant scarf from a tiny piece of cloth sticking out of his fist, inch by inch, until it was as long as the dining room table. He pulled coins from behind heads too, and revealed the card someone chose from the middle of the deck after he shuffled it twice. But his biggest trick was the one with the rings.

He lifted a stack of metal rings from his stand and held them up for everyone to see. "It's impossible to break solid steel rings, isn't that right?"

Everyone nodded.

Dad gripped the rings in one hand and started wrestling them over his head, making them clang and jangle like crazy bells. I'd seen this trick a million times. He'd wrangle them until they became different shapes, and everyone would go *aah* and *ooh* and clap.

The first shape Dad made was a porch swing. It swayed back and forth, and everyone applauded. Then the swing disappeared, and he banged the rings together again. A minute later, a butterfly emerged. The wings opened and closed slowly. Then the butterfly collapsed into a bunch of loud ringing metal until a round sphere appeared. For the last shape, Dad folded his long body into a semi crouch and placed the sphere on top of his shoulder. "I'm Atlas, carrying the weight of the world!"

It was a corny line, but I laughed anyway.

When the party was over, I found Dad in the kitchen.

"They aren't really solid, are they?" I asked. I wanted to be his accomplice and share at least one of his secrets. I remembered the night he had brought out the Viet Cong flag and told me what it meant. He had trusted me with something important then. I wanted that feeling again, that kind of confidence.

But he deflected. It was as if he was Houdini, dangling over rushing river waters wrapped in chains, and not Dad standing on linoleum kitchen tiles eating chocolate cake.

"Magicians never give away their secrets."

It's what he said every year.

But this time, I took it as a challenge. If he wouldn't share his secrets with me, maybe I'd figure them out myself. I went searching for his stand and found it in an upstairs closet. I swung open the lid and saw that it was all there: the golf balls, decks of playing cards, the small cube that held a compressed scarf, and the stack of rings. I picked one up and found a narrow break, a place where another ring could easily pass through. I closed the box and pushed it back into the closet. The next time I heard Dad practicing the ring trick in the den, I walked up to him.

"I know how you do it."

Dad kept working the rings, his face pressed into a grimace.

"They have breaks," I said, barely able to hear my voice over the racket.

He stopped, lowered the rings, handed one to me, and said, "Show me."

I took it and ran my fingers over the smooth, warmed metal. Nothing. I started to panic. It had to be here—a tiny break, the place that could open and let another ring through. Where was it? I searched again but couldn't find anything. *It's the wrong ring,* the voice scolded. Even when I had found out his trick—nearly proven it—he kept to his secrets. And kept me out. I handed the ring back, feeling as small as the break I couldn't find. And just as inconsequential.

***

The old Dad made time for me and shared things with me, the one before Vietnam. But not anymore. I started to tuck myself away—thoughts and feelings, stories and poems, including a poem about an old dog who died in his sleep—all hidden in my own secret notebook.

Not long after I started writing stories, I heard Dad call Skylos in from the yard.

I knew they'd go up by Jupiter Road, where they always walked, but I had a bad feeling. Skylos was strong and always protected us. His dark eyes watched everything. He and Dad walked after work some days. They walked side by side. Skylos didn't need a leash. This time, I wanted to tell them both to stay home. *Say something,* the voice urged. It wasn't the sharp voice I heard. It was another, deeper one, but I said nothing. Skylos's nails clipped across the tiled entryway until the front door closed behind him.

Dad came into my room the next morning, in a hurry as always. The room filled with cinnamon aftershave.

"He got hit, honey. I put him in the car and went to the vet, but it was too late."

I felt sick. Why hadn't I listened to myself and told Dad not to take him for a walk? I kept my words to myself instead, and now look what happened. The connection between the real Skylos, the dead Skylos, and the Skylos from my poem thrummed inside me. Something about writing felt strange and powerful.

The next day, I showed my poem to my sixth-grade teacher, who wore khaki skirts and had perfectly feathered blonde shoulder-length hair. She said there was a writing contest in a children's magazine and that I should enter. I liked that she had confidence in me. She sent my poem off. I forgot about it, but months later, she came to talk to me at recess.

"I want to show you something." She handed me a letter. Right away, I found my name and the words *honorable mention*.

My heart skittered, and I shoved the letter and my poem into my back pocket.

When I got home, Dad was in the den, reading from a stack of files. His vanilla-scented pipe smoke filled the room. I hadn't seen him for days. He hadn't attended my soccer game, and when Prisha came over after school, he didn't talk to us. *Don't tell him*, a voice warned. I pulled the paper from my back pocket.

"Dad?"

He looked up and squinted.

I told him my poem had won honorable mention and handed him the paper. Even if he didn't share things with me, I still could. Maybe my poem could somehow bring us together. It's what I wanted, why I went into the den to find him.

Dad took the paper with my poem and started to read. He breathed through his pipe, sliding the stem back and forth across his teeth. Clack, clack, clack. Maybe he'd like it. Maybe he'd say it was the best poem he'd ever read and ask me to read it out loud. I was so lost in my fantasies that I almost missed his response.

"Good," he said, his mouth turned down.

He handed back my poem and returned to his files. Had he even read it? When I sought him out and showed him something

I was proud of, it didn't work. We weren't any closer than before. I left the room feeling as if it never happened, as if I hadn't won honorable mention after all.

***

Months later, Dad made an announcement. "We're taking a trip to the coast to meet my brother—your uncle Tom—and his kids."

I wondered what he wasn't telling us. Why, all of a sudden, were we seeing cousins we hadn't visited in years? Maybe it had something to do with Mom being back in chemo. He said she wouldn't be coming with us.

As Dad drove toward the coast, I tried to recall the details of my uncle's face. It had been too long, and I couldn't picture him. So it was all the more shocking when we got to the motel and I saw he was a hippie. It was 1977, and I was used to seeing longhairs walking on the side of the road with guitars and satchels. Still, I didn't think they had anything in common with my family. Until now. My jaw dropped because my uncle had a beard and both he and his new wife wore bell-bottom jeans.

Dad and Uncle Tom seemed matter-of-fact with each other. One of Tom's daughters was twelve like me and blonde. The other was a year older and had dark hair. The boy was Evelyn's age and just as thin. Everyone had blue eyes but me. After saying our hellos, the five of us bolted out to the motel pool. We cannonballed from the diving board for hours. It was fun to have cousins again. Later that day, after the pool closed, Evelyn and I asked to visit our cousins in their motel room.

"Sure!" Dad said brightly.

Evelyn and I made our way to our cousins' room. We arrived and knocked on the door. Someone opened it, but I couldn't see who because the room was dark, the blinds pulled low. We stepped inside, and I could sort of make out a figure in a chair in the middle of the room. Everyone sat around them, talking and laughing. It was my uncle's wife, my cousins' stepmother. She looked like a movie star, with one slender and perfectly smooth leg draped over the arm of her chair. Her blonde hair was long and shiny. She talked and laughed and carried on as if everything was normal, except it wasn't normal because she was totally and completely naked. Evelyn and I looked at each other in disbelief. No one sat nude in a chair in our house. Just then, my uncle passed through the room and laughed. My cousins laughed. Everyone seemed in on the joke. I envied their togetherness.

That's how I want to feel, I thought. *Free.*

But the week came to an end, and along with it, my chance to know my cousins. Everything went back to the way it was before the visit. My hippie uncle and his easygoing family disappeared like Dad's golf ball trick. Abracadabra, and they were gone.

***

After living in Dallas for three years, we moved again. This time back to Northern Virginia. Instead of moving during the summer, we moved in the middle of the school year. It was winter and dark. I felt numb, like I'd lost another piece of my life. Relocating every couple of years was harder for Evelyn. She was quiet. Just when she'd made a new friend, it was time to leave again. We stayed at a dingy motel for over a month, waiting to find a house. There was no privacy inside the small space. After school, at night, I masturbated inside the overly bright bathroom. *This is wrong.* The voice loved to judge. But it was the only thing that felt good, so I did it anyway. Our family's strained energy was loud inside the single shared room. Even as no one spoke about it. It was the loudness of all that wasn't spoken. I didn't know what was causing all the stress—was Dad's stress from work and Mom's from cancer? All I knew was that I felt the pressure to adjust to a new school and a new set of peers. And that none of us talked about what we felt. It all pressed us down.

Eventually, Dad found a house, and we moved out of the motel.

On Sundays, we piled into the car for our family ritual. At thirteen, I hated these Sunday drives. They were always the same. Dad steered the car down tranquil tree-lined streets, and Mom looked out the window and commented on which yard was nicest. But on this particular day, something felt off. Dad gripped the wheel extra tightly, and Mom didn't say anything about the well-groomed lawns. I stared at the canopy of trees above the road, thinking how weird this felt, when Mom blurted out, "Tell the girls what you do for a living, Michael."

Dad's neck went stiff.

I stared at the side of Mom's face. I couldn't believe she was bringing this up, the secret topic, the one we never talked about.

"I'm a supervisor. I manage people," he mumbled.

Mom whirled around and said to me and Evelyn, "Do you girls have any questions for your father about his work 'managing people?'"

I loved the tone in Mom's voice. It was a tone that said, I've had enough of your secret, of this life of moving, of silences. It was exciting to be trusted too. It was as if our opinions mattered. I was looking at a new mother. If she could be brave, maybe I could too. Her nerve cheered me, and I jumped in with my own questions.

"What do the people you manage do?" I asked.

"Gather information."

"What kind of information?"

"Different kinds."

Mom kept her face turned toward Dad, listening to his answers. I felt like we were a team, me and Mom and Evelyn.

"What topics?" I asked.

"Events of the day, various things."

"*Which* events?" I wanted to find a way to make him say more, but his words stayed slippery.

"World events," he said.

I rolled my eyes. Mom saw Evelyn and I were about to give up. She narrowed her eyes, pursed her red lipstick lips, and said with total authority, "You work for the CIA, don't you?"

The CIA? I'd heard the word before on the news. My next thought was *spy*. It meant he was a spy. My mind flashed to the James Bond movies we watched together in the living room—*From Russia with Love, Doctor No*. Bond was a spy. He lived an exciting life of danger and heroics. He shot bad guys from helicopters, sprinted down alleys, ascended stairways, and leaped from rooftop to rooftop. When he wasn't running or shooting, he was vacationing with models on yachts or at resorts in the Swiss Alps. He wore elegant suits, smoked inside European cafes, and drove sexy sports cars.

Dad was nothing like 007. He bought American cars, wore horn-rimmed glasses, and did magic tricks. I'd never seen him run. I couldn't imagine him shooting from a helicopter or yacht, either. Dad was a nerd. How could he be a spy?

Dad's cheeks turned red, and he held onto the steering wheel as if it was all that kept him from flying from the car. A part of me felt sorry for him. But another part of me was angry. Everything wrong in our lives was because of his job—our constant moving, Mom's unhappiness, my hiding who I was, Evelyn shutting herself away. I knew my life would have been different if he had been different. At least there was a name for it now. CIA. The secret was finally out in the open.

A warm sensation spread across my chest. It was freeing, and I wanted it to keep spreading. I wanted everything to be out in the open—Mom's cancer, my liking girls, everything—but we weren't that kind of family. The moment passed. No one said anything for the rest of the ride. Dad kept his eyes on the road, and the rest of us stared out our windows. None of us mentioned this revelation the following day, week, or month either. It was as if it had never happened.

4. Trust Yourself

We dropped the subject of Dad's work after the car ride, but that didn't stop Mom from bringing up other taboo topics. One day, she sat me down at the oblong, cherry-stained, 1950s-era wooden table in the kitchen, an arrangement of pink gladiolas in the center, and told me that it was okay to masturbate.

I stared at her fingernails, thick and ridged from radiation treatments.

"It's natural, and I don't want you thinking it's bad."

But masturbation *was* bad. Or at least the way I did it was. And if Mom knew that I masturbated all the time—and that I did it with *her* sex toy—she definitely would not have approved.

It all started with *Bonanza*.

In the middle of some horse-riding scene, a thick band of horizontal lines suddenly cut across the screen.

"What's going on with the picture?" I asked Dad.

"It'll come back on soon," he said, slouched in his chair, hand deep inside a red bag of Doritos.

He was right. Fifteen minutes later, the fuzzy lines disappeared, and a clear picture returned. But when it happened again on another day, I left the den and went upstairs. I stood outside Mom's room and heard a soft buzzing coming from the other side of the closed door. *That's it,* I thought. *That's what wrecks the picture on the television.*

When Mom left the house for a medical appointment a few

days later, I snuck into her room and opened her underwear drawer. There it was: The Hitachi Magic Wand. I took it out of its box, plugged it in, and dropped onto the bed. It was hard to relax at first, my ears on constant alert for Mom's car pulling up to the house or someone else coming up the stairs, but after a bit it became easier, and I came so quickly. *I don't even have to masturbate myself*, I thought. *The wand does it for me!*

That was months before.

Not long after our talk about masturbation, Mom brought up my period. "When you get it, you'll be a woman," she said. "We'll celebrate, and I'll buy you a gift." She lifted her teacup and smiled a happy Mom smile at me.

"Okay," I said, marveling at how she kept bringing up topics that made most people, including me, squirm. The idea of getting a present just because I had started my period seemed different, but in a good way.

Months later, I was out night-jogging, trying to lose some pounds, and I felt a twinge in my abdomen. A car rounded the bend, and I put up my arm against the beam from its headlight. The twinge passed, so I jogged up to the middle school, looped it, and headed back home. In the upstairs bathroom, I took off my sweatpants and found a small, ruddy-looking smear on the crotch of my underwear. It looked tentative and weak. *Great*, I thought. *A weird period.* The next morning, it looked like proper blood. I told Mom about it. She brought in one of her Kotex pads, an enormous soft brick.

"No way," I said. "No one uses those."

Mom dragged herself to the store to get tampons.

"I had to use a pad and belt contraption when I was your age," she said, lifting the pink and blue box from the paper bag. I flashed back to our conversation about the gift, but Mom said she needed to lie down, so I decided to skip it.

***

Mom talked about risqué subjects but not about cancer. None of us did. It was getting worse. A sad pall hung over our house. To escape my sadness, I fled to my new best friend's house. Sandy had curly blonde hair, a swimming pool in her backyard, and a Lebanese mother who made delicious lamb meatballs. We lay next to each other at night during sleepovers.

"Do you think Chad likes me?" Sandy asked.

I stared at her hair carefully tucked under gray bobby pins. I loved her. I knew I wasn't supposed to, but I did.

"Of course," I said. "You're beautiful."

I wanted to say more, but the voice shushed me. We were so close I could have easily rolled over and kissed her, and I thought about doing that. But what I really wanted was for the kiss to happen without my having to say or do anything. I wasn't the one she wanted, but I basked in our closeness anyway, the fact that it was *me* she was whispering to in the dark, even if I knew the moment wouldn't last.

"I think David likes you," she said, mentioning a 9th-grade boy from my geography class. "Do you want me to send him a note?"

"Maybe," I said.

Sandy was excited.

In the hallway the next day, Sandy treated me like a sidekick. The intimacy of her bedroom was gone. We passed Chad's math class on our way to lunch.

"Go look. Tell me if you see him," she said.

I peeked through the little glass window. Chad was there with his dark brown hair swept to the side in perfect '70s disco style. He noticed me, and I ducked down.

"He saw me," I said, rushing over to Sandy.

She blushed so hard I could almost imagine it was me she was blushing for. She took the lip gloss from her back pocket and rolled on a new layer.

"How's your mom?" she asked.

"Okay. She has to buy a wig this weekend," I said.

Sandy gave me a pitying look, but I didn't mind.

***

The walls of the wig shop were miles high and lined with rows of white Styrofoam heads. Empty eyes stared out of each mannequin. Mom scanned the heads, looking for one with a wig that matched her usual look—a thick, dark brown bob that sat just above her shoulders. She tried on one after another, gazing at herself in the long mirror the way she did at her dressing table. Evelyn and I slumped in chairs. We didn't look at each other because if we did, we would have had to acknowledge how depressing it was to be there. We kept our sadness to ourselves. We pretended it was normal to be a teenager in a wig shop with our mother, a mother who was shopping for wigs because she had lost all her hair to chemo.

In the middle of my freshman year, I got my learner's permit and began driving Mom to her chemo appointments. After one of her treatments, she returned to the car, her face paler than usual. I drove us home and pulled up to the house just as the winter sun was setting. When I parked, Mom didn't make a move to leave the car. I remembered the last time she had come home from chemo. She sat in the living room throwing up into a metal mixing bowl.

Mom stared now at the leafless tree in the vacant lot next door.

"Aren't we getting out?" I asked.

She turned her face to me. "There's something I want to tell you. A couple of years ago, those doctors didn't believe me when I first felt that lump, but I knew it was there. Six weeks later it was much bigger." Her eyes shone with intensity. I stilled my breathing. She was talking to me like an adult, like I could handle things.

34

"Trust yourself. Don't let *anyone* tell you what you know." Her pale cheeks were beacons inside the darkening car. She turned back to the lone tree.

A moment later, we got out of the car and went into the house. I thought about the doctors for the rest of the night, the ones who didn't listen and let the cancer grow. I thought, too, about what Mom told me, how I should always listen to myself. I decided I would try. Even if I didn't fully trust myself in that moment, I felt the urgency of what she was saying—for her life and for mine. If those doctors had been there, standing in front of me, I would have kicked their teeth in. But really, the only power I exercised was making sure the dishes got done after dinner, which is what I did.

***

Instead of talking to me about Mom's cancer, Dad focused on education. One day, out of the blue, he said, "If you don't start bringing home books, you're going to private school." He was standing in the kitchen sorting through the mail.

I felt blindsided. It wasn't like him to notice me or the fact that my homework was easy enough to do in class. My neck turned hot.

"I don't want to change schools," I said.

I was furious with the way he casually threatened to change my life but was sure the threat would blow over. I was bringing home what he expected—mostly A's, so what was the big deal? In a few days, I figured he would forget all about me and get caught up in work. I kept finishing my homework in class and leaving books in my locker.

Weeks later, he was going through the mail again and said, "You have an interview at a private girls' school." I heard the "girls' school" part and panicked. I didn't think about boys or about dating them, but at least in public school I had the chance of some day being normal. If I went to a school with no boys, I was doomed.

I worked myself up into a state and cried uncontrollably at Mom's dressing table. She had bigger problems, I knew, but my tears kept coming.

"Maybe this isn't such a good idea," I overheard her telling Dad downstairs.

Good, I thought. Mom was on my side.

But Dad just said, "She'll adjust."

I hated him for saying this, for not caring how I felt.

On the day of the scheduled interview, I refused to talk in the car. I slumped against the passenger side door and stared out the window. But when we arrived at the campus with its manicured lawns and Colonial-styled dormitories, I switched. I couldn't stop myself; it was automatic. Instead of saying, "I don't want to attend your stupid snobby prep school that will doom me from ever having a boyfriend," I smiled like my southern belle Mom had taught me to do and said, "I like it here." I had learned how to keep the surface smooth and calm.

When I was accepted, I resigned myself to the fact that I wouldn't be seeing Sandy as often in the coming year. I called to tell her that I had to change schools but that we'd still have the weekends. I said this thinking especially about the overnights.

"We can still hang out by the pool, and Ma will make your favorite Lebanese meatballs," she said, totally missing the point.

I didn't care about her mom's food. I cared about her.

Besides ruining my chances of having a boyfriend, the worst thing about my new school was the preppy clothes the students wore. No one wore painter's pants, makeup, or Nike sneakers like me. Instead, they donned polo shirts with little alligators, khaki pants, and leather boat shoes called Top-Siders. One day, I met a Greek-American girl with long brown hair. Despina wore Converse sneakers and Army fatigues. She was a day student like me and not a boarder. We sat talking on a circle of grass in the center of campus.

I told her I used to live in Greece.

"Greeks are crazy," she said. "My parents fight about everything."

Despina talked openly about her feelings. She didn't hide them the way I did. It was a relief to be around someone who didn't hold back. I wanted to tell her my problems at home, the way she told me hers, but that heavy curtain was always there, stopping me.

Instead, we talked about how much we hated our curvy bodies.

"I am so tired of this fat," I said, looking down at my belly pushing against the waistline of my jeans.

"Me too," she said.

We compared weight-loss approaches. I told her about a strawberry-flavored powder drink I used instead of food sometimes, a product Grandmother suggested I try. Whereas I used a liquid diet, Despina took a no-food approach. Together we starved, binged, and complained. It bonded us. Neither of us could see that our relationship with food mirrored the one we had with our families. And ourselves. That no amount of starving or binging could help us accept our bodies.

Changing my externals became the way I tried to feel better on the inside. Dieting was one method; cleaning was another. One night, while I crouched in the upstairs bathroom, a bottle of cleanser and a roll of paper towels in my hands, Dad rushed into the house. *Where had he been?* He saw me but didn't ask why I was cleaning so late at night. Instead, he bolted downstairs to his office. A second later, he was upstairs again.

"I have to go out," he said, his upper lip tight with tension.

I kept on scrubbing dirty tiles.

He stopped, then, for just a moment. Maybe he saw the need on my face. I felt like he almost saw me, the real me, crouched on the floor and on the verge of tears from all the loneliness and sadness pushed down inside me. Maybe he wanted to say more, ask why I looked so upset, or how it was going at my new school.

The moment passed, and his mind snapped back to its usual whirling.

"I don't want anyone picking up the phone while I'm out. Whatever you do, don't answer it. You got that?"

I nodded and aimed the spray into a hard-to-get corner. My younger self might have been more curious. She might have wondered about Dad's secret job and how this clue fit into it all. But not teenage me. Nothing about his phone call promised me any kind of relief. Why didn't he stay home and deal with the call himself? I kept swiping at the dirt. I had my own problems. You'd think he could see this, but I guess he couldn't. The phone never rang.

***

Even though the girls at my school wore preppy clothes and no makeup, I kept dressing the way I had at public school. I was standing in front of the mirror one morning, smudging on powder blue eye shadow, when Mom popped into the bathroom.

"Get your things. We're going to San Antonio," she said, a manic look in her eye. "I'm leaving your father."

Dad popped his head into the bathroom. "Get ready for school."

Then they both left, and I heard yelling from their room.

"What is this?" Mom's voice was weirdly high-pitched.

"You know what it is." Dad's voice was rational, commanding.

I moved to the doorway of their room and saw Mom shaking a ballpoint pen at Dad.

"No, what is *this*?" It was as if they were having an argument about something else. Like the pen was standing in for a different object. Mom looked confused too, like she didn't know what a ballpoint pen was.

Dad noticed me. "I told you—get ready for school."

"You're not listening," Mom said. She threw the pen hard at

the floor. It spiked up and hit the wall. Then, she picked up the suitcase sitting on the edge of the bed and walked past me down the hall. I followed her, but I didn't know what we were doing. She got to my room and ordered me to put in some clothes. I looked at the suitcase. The only thing inside it was the canvas for a needlepoint rug Mom was working on. Forest green threads spilled out from the half-zippered bag. I felt like there were 100-pound weights tied to my arms, keeping me from raising them. I stared at Mom while she jerked a drawer open and started stuffing my T-shirts and jeans into the suitcase. Then, she zippered it closed and dashed across the hall to Evelyn's room. Evelyn put in a pair of jeans and a couple of T-shirts and glared at me as if I was being mean to Mom. *She's not okay*, I wanted to say.

Mom zipped the bag shut and headed toward the stairs.

"We need to get you to the doctor's," Dad said.

Mom ignored him and started for the stairs, followed by Dad, me, and Evelyn. We got to the first floor, and Dad pulled a small piece of paper from his pocket and turned to the wall phone. Mom lunged at him. They wrestled for the paper. Dad held his hand high in the air. His tie swung as he struggled to keep the paper away from her. They didn't talk. They groaned like animals, breath jagged, words stifled inside their throats.

Mom got a hold of the paper and tore some of it away. She whirled around and made a break for the hallway bathroom. Dad pressed from behind, his arm reaching, but it was too late. The paper hit the water, and Mom jammed down hard on the flush lever. The doctor's number disappeared inside the swirling water.

"C'mon, girls," Mom crowed.

She bolted from the house, and Evelyn and I followed. The three of us marched down the sidewalk toward the road that led out of our development.

"Where are we going?" I asked.

"Hold your shoulders back when you walk. Stop slouching."

Cars slowed to peer at the upset-looking woman dragging

a huge canvas suitcase and two teenage girls. *This is fucked up,* I thought. One car slowed but didn't pass. It stayed with us, trailing. I looked back and saw it was Dad. He looked desperate. His worried eyes locked with mine. *Stay with her,* they said. I felt like I was a little kid again and wanted to cry.

We arrived at the shopping center a half mile away and went inside. Mom strode over to the pay phone. "Ladies first!" she barked at the man who was in the middle of a call. He looked at me. I circled a finger near my temple and mouthed "crazy." Evelyn gave me a sharp look. The man hastily hung up, and Mom took his place.

"I want the number for the Yellow taxi company," Mom told information. She called the dispatcher and ordered a cab to the airport.

We went outside to wait. I scanned the parking lot for Dad's Chevrolet. Mom watched for the taxi. I didn't want it to come. If it did, she'd make us get in, and then what? We'd be on our way to the airport, and Dad would have no idea that we'd left the shopping center. He'd think we were inside the store and would search up and down, but we'd be long gone. What if we got to the airport and Mom got in trouble there and did things I couldn't control?

I slipped back into the store. My hands trembled as I picked up the hard, plastic receiver. "No one's going to the airport," I told the taxi dispatcher.

I joined Mom and Evelyn back outside, but Mom was onto me. She glared and shook her head. "Stay here. Don't move," she said.

She went into the store to call the taxi. A moment later, she was back outside, but it was too late. A police cruiser with flashing lights pulled up, and I saw Dad's car. Mom's eyes sharpened. The cop escorted her into a nearby office. He had a clipboard of questions she refused to answer.

"My religion is none of your business," she said, seething.

It was embarrassing to hear her talk back to a policeman. It was confusing too. She wasn't the polite, proper Mom I was used to. Still, why should she answer his questions? And so what if she wanted to leave Dad? That didn't seem so crazy. But walking along the highway, lugging a suitcase did. Feelings collided inside me. Evelyn slumped in a chair, her hair falling like a sheet across her eyes. I watched Mom refuse to answer another round of the policeman's questions. She looked lost and resolute at the same time. Like she was done with all the happy pretending. I was looking at my real mother now. The underneath one.

***

Mom went to the hospital for a couple of nights. Dad explained that she had had an adverse reaction to one of her medications but would be home soon. He said all this sitting across from me at the kitchen table. He lingered there every evening after dinner while she was away. He seemed softer than usual. It was comforting to talk, even if we didn't say anything that important.

And when Mom returned, our kitchen talks continued.

"How's your mother? Was she herself today?" he asked one evening as we shared a row of iced oatmeal cookies.

I told him she'd been her regular self.

"She has another appointment next week," he said. "Can you drive her?"

"Sure," I said.

It was as if I had my father back. He had salt and pepper hair now, but he was the old Dad, the one who taught me the breathing trick in the pool. He took off his glasses and rubbed his eyes, which, without lenses in front of them, were small as a bird's. And sad too. I saw the worry in them, the fact that he couldn't make Mom better either. I forgot about my anger and all the ways he didn't notice me. He saw me now. That's what mattered. I wanted to hold onto this feeling as long as I could because I knew it wouldn't last. In a few days, work would take over, and when he got home, he'd go straight downstairs to his office and stop coming to the kitchen. Which is exactly what happened.

Not long after our talks stopped, Dad asked Grandmother to come help out.

I didn't know how she could help, but it was already decided.

Dad picked her up from the airport, dropped her off at home, and then headed back out to the store. Ten minutes later, he returned with a liter bottle of vodka in a brown paper bag. "It's for your grandmother," he said, keeping his eyes down.

Grandmother, who Evelyn and I had taken to calling "Ole G.A." when she wasn't around, slept on the foldout sofa downstairs and made dinner every night. She wore skirts every day, like always, and after supper, made herself a couple of vodkas with tonic water. Her drinks transformed her from a stern person into a kind and relaxed one. She would pat the sofa beside her and tell me to come sit down. I'd drop onto the velvet seat cushion, and she would smile and say, "Tell me about your day." I could feel her love then.

One night, Ole G.A. fell down the last few stairs that led to the TV room. Dad took her to the hospital, where they put her arm in a cast. When she returned, we didn't talk about what happened, even though we all knew why she'd broken her arm. It was just another thing we didn't talk about.

5. Gone

I was a sophomore in high school when Mom started using a walker because the cancer had spread. Instead of talking about it, we stuck to our routines: Dad watched TV, Mom rested in bed, Evelyn stayed in her room, and I listened to Billy Joel records in the living room. One day, flipping through Dad's collection, I came across a Greek album. I slid the vinyl out of its paper sleeve, placed silver earphones over my ears, and lowered the needle. The bouzouki strings jangled, transporting me back to the days when I played for hours in my yard in Old Psychiko. I remembered the simple well-being I felt then—so different from how bogged down my life had become—and wondered if I would ever feel as light as that again.

That year, Grandfather died of a stroke. He had been living in an assisted living facility in San Antonio. Dad told me in the morning, bending over the kitchen table.

"My father died," he said. His eyes clouded over, but his body stayed upright.

We didn't say more. Dad's sadness stayed private and internal, but I sensed it anyway.

***

The next year, I became a boarding student. I don't remember moving into the dorm or the day I first met my roommate. She was kind, though: I remember that. What stays with me is a feeling of dislocation. Evelyn was still at home with Dad and Mom. I was five miles away, but it felt like I was on the other side of the moon. I had been heading down the path of not processing my feelings for months and years. But as Mom got sicker, my emotions became even less known to me.

Mom returned to the hospital in autumn. Dad started showing up at school unannounced. He didn't say why he was picking me up and taking me and Evelyn to visit Mom; he just appeared, and we went.

I was in the backseat during one of these quiet rides when it hit me: Mom wouldn't be coming home with new meds or plans for another surgery. I stared at the trees along the George Washington Parkway and imagined the twisting leaves were waving, trying to comfort me. It didn't occur to me to say anything to Dad or my sister. I sat alone with what I knew.

When I saw Mom, I faked it and acted like everything was okay.

"How's my maroon girl," she said, seeing me in my wine-colored sweater.

"Pretty good," I said and smiled back.

A few days later, a kind woman named Lois, the wife of one of Dad's work friends, picked me up and drove me to the hospital. She said Dad and Evelyn were already there.

When we arrived, Lois dropped me off at the entrance, and I rushed into the lobby.

Mom's best friend, a tall woman with shoulder-length brown hair, stood by the elevators. "Hurry," she said.

I skipped the elevator and took the stairs. My heart resounded inside my chest as I took two at a time. I counted the floors as I went, stopped for a second on the third floor, and then kept going. On the fifth floor, I flung open the door and started to sprint down the gray corridor tiles. People stared, but I didn't care. I had to get to Mom. At the end of the hall, my footsteps exploded into her room, and I saw Dad and Evelyn. Tears streamed down their cheeks. I had never seen Dad cry so freely, his face broken open.

Mom lay unmoving on the bed. Her eyes were closed, but her head was turned toward the door, as if she had tried to wait for me, as if she hadn't wanted to go before saying goodbye. I reached for her hand; it was cool and still.

There would be no more hospital visits. No more talks at the kitchen table or in the car after chemo appointments. A thousand unspeakable words rose up in my throat, words I couldn't yet reach, words I would spend the rest of my life forming and unforming.

But in that moment, all I wanted was for us to stay together. To stand next to Mom's body and be with her this one last time.

Instead, Dad sent me back to school.

I crumpled down in the passenger seat next to Lois as tears slid down my cheeks. They were small tears. My other tears were locked deep inside, and it would take years to unlock them.

Back on campus, my friends threw their arms around me and looked sadly into my eyes. One of my teachers walked with me around campus and said, "This is a hard time, but you'll get through it." I didn't know how this could be true.

After Mom died, I remember taking a shower in the mornings before school and thinking that my life felt far away. I had no idea how to process her death. I went through the motions of going to class and seeing Dad and Evelyn on weekends. Mostly, I remember being lost.

***

A few weeks later, inside a cemetery chapel in San Antonio, Mom's closed casket was covered with white calla lilies. Dad wore one of his dark work suits. Uncle Tom and a woman he had recently married named Linda—a petite woman with long auburn hair—were there. I had met her during a brief visit to our house before Mom died. Janet and Grandmother Absher were present, along with my aunt Anne and my uncle Phil, Mom's brother. Who else was there? Friends of the family, extended family? I'm not sure. When I picture that day, I see the casket covered with flowers and then us standing outside by the grave—Linda's long hair tucked into a bun, Evelyn with her hair covering her eyes. I don't remember much more, just flashes of images and splinters of memories. Except the priest. Not his face or any of his physical features but his words. As he began to talk about God inside the little chapel, before we went to the gravesite, I tuned him out. He was talking about a God I didn't understand or believe in, and I didn't want to hear this priest's whiny voice. I stared out the small window at the headstones on the hillside, wishing I was somewhere else, when I heard him say, "Jeanette Patricia Absher has left us and gone to God's house where she'll sweep and keep house."

My attention snapped back. He was saying Mom was God's *maid*. If I could have, I would have stopped him from talking altogether. I would have taken the Bible from his hand, chucked it out the window and screamed that Mom was not some generic housewife. She was the most powerful person I knew—a brave artist who painted her deepest feelings and who tried to tell the truth.

***

That Thanksgiving, Dad sent me and Evelyn to Vermont. The roads were covered in black ice as our Greyhound bus pulled into the central Montpelier station. The all-day trip, much of it in the dark, made me feel lonely. Arriving in the dark and cold compounded the sensation.

"Great to see you guys," Tom said, twisting around and giving us a smile as we climbed in. Tom no longer looked like a hippie. He had gray hair like Dad, wore jeans, and a flannel shirt and baseball cap. The visor was pulled low, so I couldn't read his eyes. Maybe we were just a family obligation. His sister-in-law had died. His brother was busy with work, and the kids were alone at Thanksgiving. Poor girls.

Linda sat beside Tom. As soon as we got into the car, she lunged over the seat and gave us both a hug, as if she were a firefighter rushing into a burning building to save children.

"I am so sorry about your mother," she said.

Her arms encircled me, and I fought off tears.

The next morning, we came downstairs to the smell of dark roast coffee. My three cousins were there, along with Linda's two teenage sons. Everyone had long hair and talked at once as they grabbed things from the fridge. We played games and took walks, and I felt like I was in a new country.

On Thanksgiving Day, Linda cooked the turkey, and we all helped make pies, mashed potatoes, and a huge leafy salad. We gorged on food. Later, we watched a movie and ate huge bowls of popcorn sprinkled with nutritional yeast. I felt like I had become a different person in just four days. I didn't want to go back to Virginia, to the place where Mom had died, to the lonely dorm room I now shared with a girl I hardly knew. My life was in pieces. Evelyn was at a private school near home because she didn't want to go to my uptight prep school. She had said she wasn't interested during the interview so that they wouldn't accept her. Sometimes I wish I had done that too. Refused to be a good girl.

6. Sheep Story

During the months after Mom died in autumn of 1981, I hardly saw Dad. I lived at school, while Evelyn stayed alone at the house with Dad. At the end of the semester, she transferred to a boarding school in Western Massachusetts. We all lived apart after that. Instead of Virginia, where I went to private school and where we had moved several times, Vermont became home—to me at least. Evelyn and I went to Vermont for summer vacation and some holidays. I learned about the world but also about my family. Especially Dad. It started like this. Tom would be in the kitchen, pouring coffee into a mug. I would be settling in for breakfast at the wooden farm table in their cozy kitchen. A cousin or two would tumble into the room from upstairs. Tom, a poet and English professor, would tip half-and-half into his mug of coffee, take a sip, and start a story.

"In my family, we never, *ever* talked about feelings," he said.

Tom was soft-spoken, his voice not as deep as Dad's baritone, but his watery blue eyes showed they were brothers. As soon as Tom started telling a story, I was enraptured. Things like this never happened at our house. Dad didn't launch into stories about growing up. Mom didn't tell many stories either, but at least I knew about her childhood—that she had gone to St. Mary's Hall in San Antonio, a catholic girls' school, and had been an elementary school art teacher after graduating from the University of Texas in Austin. But not just where she went to school, which I knew about

Dad also, but I had heard tales about her childhood. Mom and her sister, my aunt Anne, would talk about people they knew and what was changing in San Antonio. Sometimes they told funny stories about growing up. Or my grandmother Janet would talk about what Mom was like as a child. There was a continuity. I had a sense of the artist gatherings Janet held inside their home, the big splashy Christmas parties my Great Aunt threw at her house in the hill country, the parties during San Antonio's Fiesta Week, when the daughters of old San Antonio families wore sequined gowns and sat on floats that wound through the city streets. I understood Mom much more than Dad.

So when Tom started his stories, I was hungry for information. The first one to make an impression was the sheep story.

Uncle Tom described the day Grandfather drove everyone up to hill country for summer vacation. Grandfather was behind the wheel, and Grandmother sat in her place beside him. Summer stretched out before everyone. My uncle said he couldn't wait to read a whole stack of comics. He imagined Dad felt the same way. But when the car pulled up to the cabin, Grandfather's mood changed. Tom followed Grandfather's gaze out the window and saw a flock of sheep and lambs grazing lazily on Grandfather's land. Tom said he remembered the way their tails moved back and forth like windup toys as they ate.

Grandfather turned off the engine and got out of the car. He walked to the back and opened the trunk. Tom said he knew what Grandfather was getting out of the trunk. He said they all did. Grandfather came to the front of the car and, without saying a word, braced the rifle against the car door and started shooting. Uncle Tom said the sheep scrambled toward the broken fence, colliding with one another in their rush to find the opening and escape. He and Dad watched helplessly as they dropped, one by one. Grandfather had told the neighbor the summer before to keep the sheep off his property.

"Father only warned you once," Tom explained.

This was the same grandfather who took me and Evelyn out for ice cream whenever we visited, who made jokes about being bald, who had a broad face and mostly wore tan suits, and who seemed to laugh so easily.

Everyone in the kitchen was stunned, including me.

After Grandfather had shot the sheep, Tom said that he and Dad spent the rest of the afternoon dragging heavy sheep bodies onto the neighbor's property. They replaced the missing fence boards and reset the barbed wire. Tom said that neither of them said a word.

"We had learned by then that talking only made things worse."

My uncle's story chilled me. It also informed me. I had learned more about Dad's childhood in one morning than I had ever learned from Dad. I felt as if I was meeting his family for the first time. It was a family with secrets. And a lot of silence.

My uncle said he was eager to leave Texas and that Dad had already enrolled at Exeter in New Hampshire by then, admitted as a junior. Tom didn't want to be left alone in the house, so he asked to go to prep school too. He applied to Lawrenceville and was accepted. He said it was a whole new world. Everyone talked at boarding school. A small group of students sat around a table waiting to get called on.

"The teachers would say things like, 'Mr. Absher, what do you think Hamlet meant about this or that?' They wanted to know what the students thought. That was a revelation."

When Tom and Dad came home from boarding school, they had become used to speaking their minds. They'd be at the dining room table talking about current events, and Grandfather would tell them to stop. My uncle said Grandfather objected to talking about politics.

"But really, we didn't talk about anything. It was an impropriety just to speak."

I tried to picture Dad home from boarding school, his head full of new ideas, he and Tom sitting across from each other at my grandparents' formal dining room table, wanting to express themselves but unallowed. I saw the fire dim in Dad's eyes and watched his shoulders slump.

My uncle told other stories that shed light on their childhood. He said they had grown up in a big house on Divine Road in San Antonio. It sounded fancy, like a mansion. He said Grandfather had been a wildcatter during the Depression and had originally hailed from Oklahoma. He said Grandfather didn't come from money and that when he was nineteen, Grandfather's own father had died in a barnyard accident. In an instant, Grandfather had become responsible for his mother, sister and brother. He paid his own way through college by working as a telegraph operator for the railroad companies, graduated with a geology degree, and became a geologist. Then he started buying mineral rights in different places.

I started to see Grandfather in a new light. He wasn't just cruel. He was resourceful too.

My uncle said oil was struck on one of Grandfather's plots. That's what really got things going. He made money from that strike and a few others. Grandfather wanted Tom and Dad to take over the business, manage the money from these oil strikes, but neither brother wanted to do that. They were going in different directions. Tom said boarding school had ignited different passions in each of them.

Still, Uncle Tom said he loved that big house on Divine Road. He would come home from school and sit downstairs with a glass of milk and read comics for hours. The house was empty and silent.

"Mike was usually upstairs in his room, practicing magic tricks in front of the long mirror."

I pictured teenage Dad, tall and lanky like everyone else in the Absher family, studying himself in the mirror as he practiced sleight of hand tricks over and over again. I imagined him shuttling the golf ball from one palm to the other, struggling to conceal the switch inside hands not yet big enough to do it.

***

Linda, a poet and feminist, told me stories too. She shared them as we walked the fields behind their house, our boots crunching the nearly frozen grass. One afternoon, she told me something about Ole G.A. that made me stop in my tracks: she had been married before Grandfather. Linda said she had fallen in love with someone her own mother disapproved of, and instead of calling off their relationship, they eloped. But the relationship didn't last, and Grandmother later married Grandfather. I tried to imagine Ole G.A. as young and impulsive, who once made a decision that went against convention. I recalled the person I knew and saw still whenever I traveled to San Antonio—stern and sometimes warm, who had kept the fridge supplied with Eskimo pies for our summer visits when we were little, after we left Greece. She also told me how she had disciplined herself not to eat potatoes in order to keep weight off when she was a teenager. She told me this as a warning against gaining weight. Grandmother—Ole G.A.—was headstrong and commanding. I wondered who this first husband was as I imagined her secret life before Grandfather.

We came to a dirt road imprinted with frozen tire ruts, crossed it, and entered the next field. I had to work to keep pace with Linda. Small as she was and clad in heavy work boots ("shit kickers," she called them) and a dark green down coat, Linda was fast. As we made our way across the winter ground, Linda told me another story about Grandmother.

She said that growing up, Dad and Tom had quintessential little boy rooms full of comics and decoder rings and train sets. One day, while they were at school, Grandmother went into their rooms and cleared them all out. She got rid of everything. She threw out the comics, the Army men, and all the special mail-order toys. She bought new rugs and lamps.

Linda said, "She erased it all."

***

It dawned on me that, until now, I had known little about my father's childhood, or really any of his past. It had been a hidden world. Not anymore. His silence made sense to me now. So did mine. Already, I felt Vermont changing that, changing me. Uncle Tom, Linda, my cousins, everyone talked about everything here: feminism, smoking pot, American imperialism. At first, it felt shocking to criticize U.S. foreign policy out loud. I had somehow developed a left-leaning political point of view on my own, and I wasn't used to saying it out loud. Dad was a Republican, and Mom seemed apolitical. Maybe I developed it to spite him. Or maybe it was the world changing around me. In Vermont, it was fine to criticize the U.S. government, to deconstruct capitalism. Everyone criticized Reagan, especially his economic theory promising that money at the top somehow "trickles down" to everyone else. Linda was outspoken but so was everyone, including my cousins. They seemed worldly and informed. No topic was too controversial or off-limits, except for one. Dad's job. No one brought it up. When Dad called my uncle to check in, they talked from the other room. Tom's voice was low, serious. There was a respect in his tone.

Not mentioning Dad's work felt familiar. It was part of being a good daughter, something I felt in my bones without anyone having to tell me. If I thought about his job at all, I pictured him at a desk. What was he reading or who was he talking to? I imagined him having heated discussions about the threat of the Soviet Union to the American Way of Life. Whatever he did, it was in an office. I was sure of that. But I was used to it just being me, Evelyn and Mom keeping quiet about Dad's work. Mom had said he was a spy that day in the car, but this memory didn't feel completely real to me anymore. Had I remembered it right? Had she really said that? In Vermont, I noticed it wasn't just me and Evelyn who kept silent about it. Everyone did. It was as if we had all been conscripted together.

***

Evelyn and I returned to Vermont that summer. It was the only place that made sense. We had been sent there by Dad initially, but over time it became our choice. I wanted to go. It was the only place that felt right. And if Vermont was a new kind of home, Linda was a new kind of mother. After she emerged from her writing study in the afternoons, I followed behind as she delivered kitchen table scraps to the compost heap and talked about how the patriarchy had shaped women's lives. Class politics threaded through most of her conversations. I was mesmerized.

One day, Linda asked what books I was reading. I told her I read whatever my English teacher assigned.

"You should read *The Color Purple*," she said, shaking out the bin and banging it against the black earth. "It's about an abused woman who finds her way to recovery."

Back at the house, she handed me a copy of *Diving into the Wreck* by Adrienne Rich. She said Rich was one of the most important minds of the twentieth century. "She's also a lesbian." Linda said the word like it was ordinary, harmless, or like it might even be *good*. It shocked me to hear the word out in the open, but I pretended it didn't. I wanted to at least seem as cool as Linda.

Talk came easy to Linda. Her words flowed—about politics and literature, but about her brutal childhood too. She described her working-class background, her violent upbringing and how she had been sexually abused by her father. She was working on poems about this abuse. She shared the story of her life with me, and although sometimes her stories were like a punch in the gut, they opened me up.

"My mom had a breakdown when we came back from Greece," I heard myself say.

I started to tell Linda about the night Mom got me and Evelyn out of bed. How we sat on the sofa and watched her pace and say things that didn't make sense. I told her it was scary. I told her how the next day, we went to school as always, but when we came home from school, Mom was gone and Grandmother was there.

It felt unreal—this memory and the telling of it. Still, I kept talking.

I told Linda about how we had to live with Grandmother for two months because Mom had been admitted into the hospital and Dad was still in Vietnam. I told her how our grandparents didn't get along. I shared everything. It was like I was being a new version of myself. I didn't say things as eloquently as Linda, but she listened anyway.

"You've been through so much," she said when I was done, her light brown eyes warm.

It stunned me to hear this. She had been sexually abused, kicked around the kitchen floor like a dog, and she thought I had been through a lot. For the first time in a long time, instead of fighting my tears, I let them fall.

QUEER

7. Graduation

For my senior year of high school, I moved into a room tucked under the eaves of an old brick dorm. A girl with chestnut brown hair who lived on another floor knocked on my door and introduced herself. We talked for hours. I went to her room the next night and the one after that. Each time I crossed Dori's scuffed floorboards, her dark eyes followed me—wide and unashamed. I sat on her bed, my back against the wall, and felt her energy pulling me closer. My own desire vibrated just below the surface of my skin.

Instead of touching, we talked.

She told me she used to live in Paris, where her father had been stationed.

"He says he's with the State Department." Dori made a big point of rolling her eyes. "But State is just a cover. He's probably really in the CIA."

Dori said "CIA" casually, as if it were an everyday word like "soap" or "lawnmower."

As if she didn't consider it her duty to keep her father's secret. There was defiance in her voice too, as if she refused to keep it. How did she manage to break the family rule like that? Who gave her permission? Instead of saying any of this, I told Dori I had lived overseas too—in Greece, during a dictatorship. I said my dad had just moved to Miami and that he worked for the government doing "who knows what."

"They're probably both in the CIA," Dori said, laughing.

We talked this way every night—about our parents, school politics, and U.S. imperialism. Dori said all the U.S. did was invade other countries and install dictators. I agreed. Dori was outspoken, and talking to her every night made me loosen up. She didn't mince words about anything. The fact that we attended Madeira, a girl's school founded by a woman, but now run by a man, pissed us both off. Dori said it was because the former headmistress had killed her diet doctor lover and gone off to prison, which was an embarrassment to the school. "They brought in a man to fix things," she said.

We discussed everything but our desire. Then one night, after our words gave out, we lay facing each other on her small twin bed. I let my hand run down the slope of her hip, over the smooth, cool sheet. My breath quickened. It was the most desire I had ever let myself feel. I kept my hand above the sheet and didn't go any further. I didn't have the courage to kiss, and neither did Dori. It was enough to have her hand on my face, against my cheek, and hear her whisper, "I love you."

I returned to Dori's room every night but only at night. During the day, I chain-smoked Marlboro Lights inside the senior clubhouse with girls who had horses and charge cards to Ann Taylor. Girls who liked boys. When I passed Dori on campus, I looked away. I had perfected the trick of living a double life by then, acting normal around girls who liked boys and then switching to liking Dori when we were alone. It felt familiar, like something I had always known how to do. Just like Dad sneaking a golf ball from one hand to the next, I shuttled my feelings back and forth. If I didn't let too much show, no one would see who I really was or what I felt for Dori.

There was a girl at school who didn't keep her desire hidden the way I did. She put her arm around her best friend and didn't care what people thought. She didn't tuck away her desire like I did.

One afternoon, one of the Southern girls drew her cigarette to her lips and said with derision, "We all know what she is, don't we?" Everyone nodded. I nodded. I felt ashamed for doing it but I knew I couldn't be like her. I had no idea how to be that free.

***

When it was time to apply to college, I had no clue where to start. Linda said I should consider schools in Boston. "That's where the feminists are." She said "feminists," but I heard "lesbians."

I filled out an application to Boston University and got in.

At the end of the year, while I was packing up my room, Dori came by and gave me a card. The front cover showed an image of a man and woman ballroom dancing. I could tell by the speech bubbles Dori had added that I was the man and she was the woman.

"Don't leave me," the woman said.

"I'll never leave you," the man answered.

That summer, Dori invited me to her family's beach house. Her uncle drove while we cuddled in the backseat. I had my head resting on Dori's lap. It was a brazen thing to do and it made me uncomfortable. But I liked it too. For a split second, I tried to convince myself this was what good friends did, but I knew it wasn't true. I was about to sit up when Dori leaned down and kissed me. It was quick and furtive. My first real kiss, a kiss given in secret, in the back seat, when no one was looking.

***

Dad and Evelyn both came to my high school graduation. So did Mom's sister, my Aunt Anne. Grandmother Janet was in treatment for lung cancer and couldn't make it. In a few months, she too would be gone. My family felt fractured to me. We posed for pictures on the manicured grass and pretended we were cohesive, but we weren't. Dad, Evelyn and I used to see each other every day when we lived together. And then Mom died. Now we lived in different states. Evelyn was in a boarding school in Massachusetts, and Dad had moved to Florida. We saw each other hardly at all, over school holidays or vacations. Now that Mom was gone, nothing was the same. The person who had helped us break our family silences, who dared to say uncomfortable things, had abandoned me, leaving me with the one who clung to rules.

Dad gave me a graduation present. His gift was a trip to Europe. It was a two-week trip that he wouldn't be joining me for. Once again, he left me in the care of others. Steve, a college buddy who had grown up in Hungary, would be taking me and his teenage daughter, someone I hardly knew, to Europe. The last time I had seen Steve and his daughter was years ago, when we visited their home in New Jersey. Steve and Dad stayed up drinking past the time the rest of us wanted to leave. From the kitchen, with every shot of whiskey, their talk got louder and louder.

"Goddamned communists!" one of them shouted.

I saw my real Dad then, the way his unshakeable beliefs seemed to define him.

Now Steve was taking me and his daughter to Europe. We rented a car and drove narrow roads, and I counted the days it would be over. By the end, I liked his daughter but was sure she would have preferred to go without me. The same way I would have preferred to go with my father and not strangers.

***

When the trip was over, I flew to Miami.

The lobby of Dad's condo building had tall leafy plants, a slick marble floor, and a security guard Evelyn and I were always trying to evade. Not because we were forbidden to leave the building, but because it was something to do. We spent our afternoons by the pool. On the weekends, Dad took us driving. Tall palm trees leaned toward us as we headed to the Florida Keys. We stopped for burgers at fast food places and drank vanilla milkshakes through red straws. Sometimes we commented on the crazy South Florida outfits people wore. Mostly we ate in silence. Our familiar form of deep togetherness.

8. But We're Not

When I arrived in Boston for college, I didn't know anyone. My freshman dorm was on the seventh floor of a brick building on Beacon Street, and every afternoon my roommates and I took the elevator to the grubby lounge to watch soaps. We had just settled in for an episode of *General Hospital*, the one where Laura—young, blonde, and beautiful—had returned to her role after having left the show for two years, when someone made a wisecrack. I turned to see a girl with light brown hair and piercing blue eyes wearing an old-fashioned newsboy hat. She smiled at me. It was the kind of smile I had always been looking for. Sweat collected under my T-shirt. She seemed bold, like she was used to smiling at girls. I laughed at other people's jokes for the rest of the show but the only person I really wanted to hear was her.

I thought about her all the next day. When I got back to the dorm after class, she was in the lobby, choosing a soda from the vending machine.

"I'm Susan," she said, giving me another one of those smiles.

We talked until three a.m. that night, sitting on ratty chairs at the end of the hall. It was the same the next night, and the one after that. We argued about politics under fluorescent lights and never leaned in to kiss, never moved to touch. When I blamed capitalism for poverty, Susan countered that it wasn't all bad. She said she was a Republican and didn't believe in abortion.

"How can you be a woman and not be pro-choice?" I asked.

"It's still a life. It doesn't make me anti-woman."

I didn't know how it was that I had feelings for someone so different, so *conservative*, but I did. Susan wore ties tucked into vests and checked the stock prices in the *Wall Street Journal* every morning, whereas I enrolled in women's studies classes and stopped shaving my legs. I wanted us to agree more, but our arguments drew me out too.

A month into our late-night talks, I was in my room, asleep, when the phone rang. It was early morning and dark. I stumbled across my messy room and picked up the receiver.

"Leslie, it's me." Dad's voice sounded washed out. "Listen, I'm in Barbados. In a few hours, the U.S. is going to invade Grenada."

"Grenada?"

My roommate rolled over and squinted at me.

"I'm telling you before it hits the news. I need you to take down a number."

For a split second, I was happy. It felt exciting, to be let in. Then the feeling flickered. Our connection had gone back and forth like this all my life. It was too little, too late. I reminded myself I couldn't trust him. Still, I had questions—where was Grenada and what was *he* doing there anyway? The day Mom had outed him as a spy didn't feel fully real to me anymore. Had I remembered the moment correctly? Was I sure? A part of me wanted to know, wanted to ask him what he was doing and why, wanted to be a rebel like Mom or Linda. Instead, I did what I was told.

"Just a sec," I said and searched the floor for a pen. Dad told me the number of the Barbados Hilton where I could leave a message, and I copied it down. "Got it," I said.

"I have to go. Love you," Dad said.

"Love you too."

That evening, a bunch of us watched the news in the lounge. An internal power struggle within the island nation's communist government erupted in violence. Hundreds of American medical school students waited to be evacuated. A reporter said the students were in danger. I rolled my eyes. *More Reagan imperialism,* I thought. I told Susan that Dad was there, but I didn't tell anyone else. I watched the report and pretended I was like everyone else, hearing about a distant world event for the first time. Passing for "normal" was easy. I had been doing it my whole life—with Dad's job, Mom's cancer, and my liking girls. Still, a knot of worry tightened inside me. Was my father in danger? I was afraid to watch the news until Dad called a few days later and said he was back in Florida. I could relax again.

***

Susan and I spent all of our time together. All I wanted was to be near her, to feel her skin against mine. We lay next to each other on my bed, listening to Joan Armatrading records. I glided my index finger across her back and felt the warmth of her body through the cotton fabric of her T-shirt.

"Guess the letter," I said.

"S?" she said, guessing correctly.

I kept spelling out her name, letter by letter. My finger traveled from one side of her back to the other, touching as much of her as I could. When I was done with her name, I traced out three more words. They tumbled out of me and onto her back, one after the other. My face felt hot, but I did it anyway. I couldn't stop myself. Susan rolled over and gave me a big, gorgeous smile, and I thought, *She is mine—this woman is mine.* Then my stomach dropped. If I kept going, did what I wanted to do, then my other life, the forbidden one, would start. A life I wasn't ready to name or live. Instead of giving Susan the same look she was giving me, I offered the small lie of a smile. Friendly. Safe. I told myself it was enough. I didn't need more.

The next time Dori called, I told her I had a new friend.

"You love her more than me, don't you?"

"That's not true," I said.

But it was.

***

In addition to women's studies classes, I enrolled in Greek language classes. I sat inside small rooms with Greek-American students who had grown up speaking Greek at home. We translated Aesop's Fables, and every night I combed through my Greek-English dictionary, looking up every other word. I stumbled over the vocabulary the next day in class, but my pronunciation made me sound like a native. I thought of Dad, who spoke Greek fluently but always sounded like an American.

At the start of the second semester, Dad called to say there was someone he wanted to introduce me and Evelyn to. He flew us to Miami for spring break, and we met Cindy, a woman who lived in the condo building next door to Dad's. The four of us spent the weekend lounging around the pool. Things went okay until Dad started pontificating about the Soviet Union and communism. Cindy seemed impressed by all his knowledge and experience. Had Dad told her he was in the CIA by then? Maybe he told her but said, "My daughters don't know yet." I'm not sure. I blamed the U.S. for failed imperialism all over the world, including in Grenada, where Dad had gone—working for the State Department? The Pentagon? It didn't matter. Cindy wasn't bothered that he was part of America's imperialist efforts. She was kind to me and caring, but we didn't have the same view about Dad or the world.

For the rest of spring break, while Dad was at work, Cindy tried to get me to open up. She said it must be so difficult having lost my mother. *Uh, yeah*, I said inside my head. My tears were still locked somewhere inaccessible. My snarky self was closer. Cindy pressed on. She wanted to know why I didn't talk to Dad more often, share more of my feelings.

"Because he doesn't deserve it," I finally said.

I told her that his job had made everything harder for our family, that he never listened, and that he always made decisions unilaterally. I knew she was trying to help, but I couldn't tell if she wanted this for me or for her. It was easier for me to feel my anger toward Dad—even if I kept it inside—than it was to feel sadness over losing Mom.

***

The only one I let in was Susan.

At the Nickelodeon Theater in Boston, the floors sticky and painted black, we watched *Entre Nous*, a French movie about two middle-class housewives stuck with boring husbands. We held hands in the dark, watching the women fall in love with each other. Susan's hand felt electric inside mine. The old impulse to hide was there, but my attraction was stronger, so I left my hand where it was.

Not long after, the rumors caught up with us.

"That Goth-dressing girl on the first floor thinks we're lesbians," I said to Susan. "She's telling everyone that we're together." It stunned me to say the word.

We were standing close to each other in our usual spot at the end of the hall.

"How can she say that?" I asked. I felt exposed. Someone had noticed my feelings. My strategy had broken down. Failed. Before, I had allowed myself to have feelings for girls as long as I didn't say the word. But now, it was all out in the open, and I had no script to guide me.

"What if we were?" Susan asked. She had her hand around my waist.

"But we're not," I said, still clinging to secrecy.

Susan dropped her arm from my waist.

***

In the middle of a women's studies lecture about lesbian poets, a student with short spiky hair who wore black Doc Marten boots announced to the class that she was gay. Just like that. It was 1984, and the room went completely silent. The professor, who wore jeans and large square glasses that stayed tinted hours after being inside, invited the class to an informal post-lecture discussion about sexuality at a nearby pub.

Don't go, don't go, don't go, the voice urged. I told myself that I would have the cover of doing it for class. I imagined other students would be there too, and I could blend into the background.

I showed up at the bar wearing my signature experimental garb, a black-and-white polka-dotted skirt, and a wool WWII nurse's cape from the Army Navy store. I spotted the woman with spiky hair talking to two other women at a corner table. My palms sweat. Where was everyone?

The woman smiled when I sat down.

A moment later, our professor showed up, and one of the students said, "I wish more straight women had come." Everyone agreed. No one looked at me as if I counted as a straight woman, as if I might be anything *but* gay. They saw me as part of a club I wasn't ready to be included in. I stared at the layer of foam on my beer and tried to follow the discussion, but all I really heard was the panic ringing inside my head. Was I gay? How could I be sure? Everyone else seemed so certain about who they were, but all I felt was afraid and confused.

By the end of freshman year, my pushed-down grief over my mother's death started to seep into everything. I walked around with a hollow feeling. What day was today, tomorrow? I didn't know. I stopped going to Susan's room. No more talks until three in the morning about politics. Susan demanded to know what was happening. We sat on worn-out chairs, the rough fabric irritating my skin, and stared at each other.

"What's going on?" she asked.

I opened my mouth, but nothing came out. I couldn't explain what had changed and why I couldn't seem to find my way back to her or myself. I wanted her to know me, wanted us to be close, but I had no way of explaining that I was paralyzed. My tears ran. They burned through me. If I could have explained myself, I would have. But I couldn't. So we sat wordlessly. Susan stared at me, waiting for me to speak. I looked down at my lap with not a clue what to say.

After what felt like hours, Susan said, "I'm done with this."

She got up and walked toward the elevator.

"Don't go," I said, following behind. "Please."

The elevator arrived, and Susan stepped onto it. Something irreversible was happening. I was losing the person I loved. The elevator slid closed, and Susan disappeared. All that remained was my scratched-up reflection on the surface of the metal doors.

I pressed the button and got onto the elevator when it returned.

When I reached the lobby, Susan was gone. I hung around the dorm entrance until the security guard asked what I was doing.

"Waiting for a friend," I said, not "my best friend" or "deepest friend," nor the way I addressed her in a letter over Christmas break: "Dear Most Excellent Friend."

I walked out onto the midnight sidewalk. Music blared from the frat next door.

Fifteen minutes later, Susan reappeared.

"I want to talk," I said, desperate to preserve our intimacy.

"I have nothing to say to you," she said as she came to a stop in front of me.

We stared at each other. She leaned forward as if to kiss me, and I stepped back. She turned from me, walked away again, and then came to a stop in front of the blue mailbox near the dorm entrance.

"Why can't you just leave me alone?" she asked, her back to me.

"I'm sorry," I said, gutted by what I couldn't stop from happening.

"No, you're not."

Susan slammed both hands into the blue curved box, toppling it onto its side, all the unsent letters still inside—bills, love letters, birthday cards. I stared at what she'd done as she swept past me into our dorm lobby, feeling pain for us both and knowing there was nothing I could do about it.

***

That summer, Cindy lined up a job for me with Delta Airlines at Miami International Airport. Every morning, I slipped on a navy blue skirt and white blouse and went to work tying destination tags onto the suitcases of hurried travelers. But there were too many codes to memorize, and after a while, I started guessing. Was it Des Moines or Dallas? I didn't tell anyone when I made mistakes. What did it matter anyway? What, if anything, mattered?

Pointlessness followed me back to Boston for my sophomore year. Susan and I weren't friends anymore. We sometimes saw each other in strained moments at the dining hall or while talking with one of the friends we still had in common. Sadness at our breakup—one I seemed not to be able to change—stabbed at me.

I wandered across the Mass Avenue Bridge at night, letting the cold sear me. The sky was dark and so was the river. Students passed laughing and joking as if they were having the time of their lives. I was in college. I was supposed to be having the time of my life. Maybe I should go somewhere else, start again like I had my whole life. Maybe that would save me. Moving had been instilled in me by then. It felt automatic to think the answer lay someplace else.

I found a brochure in the campus study-abroad office, a photograph of the Parthenon on the cover. *This is it*, I thought. My Greek from class was coming along. Memories of eating at tavernas and sitting in the backyard listening to Mom tell fairy stories flooded me. *Greece is home*, I thought. More than Vermont. More than any place.

I filled out an application and told Dad.

"If that's what you want to do," he said.

One night over Christmas break, while I sat on the floor of Dad's Miami condo stuffing sweaters into my suitcase, he strode into the room, his face red with stress.

"There's something I don't want you mentioning while you're over there."

He rattled off a string of letters. Some sort of code. What was he talking about? I had never heard of this acronym, if that's what it was. He acted like he was giving me important information, but I didn't get it. And I didn't want to.

"Whatever you do, don't mention what I just said to anybody. Don't say those words. Got it?"

The expression on his face made it clear that it was for my own protection.

I wasn't interested. Not in his secrets nor his protection nor whatever this was. The whole thing made no sense. I didn't want to know about his clandestine work. My going back to Greece had nothing to do with that. I wanted no part of it. I was going back to childhood, to my Greece. Not his. I had no idea what it would feel like to be in Greece again. I was chasing ghosts, convinced the answers I was looking for and needed lay in my past.

***

I arrived in Athens after an overnight flight. The airport was instant chaos. People frantically hunted down baggage carts as cardboard boxes and canvas bags spilled from the open mouth of the carousel. Greeks piled bags on top of boxes, making pyramids they could barely see around. I grabbed my suitcase and caught a cab to the apartment where the school's director lived. She greeted me and invited me inside. When we sat down, she brought out a plastic lighter and lit a cigarette, noting that my application stated I had lived in Athens as a kid.

"What brought your family to Greece?" she asked.

I scanned my mind for something that sounded neutral. I didn't have any real information, only my suspicions that Dad— and the U.S.—had been on the wrong side of things here.

"My father worked for the government. He was stationed here."

She let out smoke slowly. "I wouldn't tell too many people that if I were you."

I was sure she knew my secret—knew more than I did, knew what Dad had done here and why. Instead of running away from him, coming here seemed to make Dad's shadow larger.

***

The program I had enrolled in was tiny and didn't have a big university building. Instead, we met for classes inside teachers' apartments. I wandered downtown streets after class. Everywhere I went, I saw anti-American graffiti scrawled across the sides of apartment buildings. One day, at a kiosk, I caught a headline from an English-language paper. The words CIA and junta blared across the top. I read on. The article said that the U.S. government had helped orchestrate a coup in 1967. It also stated that the CIA had played a role in setting up that coup, and that the coup had led to a seven-year dictatorship in which thousands were tortured or imprisoned. I panicked. We had lived in Greece while all of that had been happening. I tried to convince myself the dictatorship was over and that democracy had been restored. But it didn't feel over. The dictatorship had collapsed just ten years earlier. The pain and anger it left behind seemed alive and well. I felt it all around me.

I ran from Dad and America for the rest of the semester. I studied Byzantium and memorized the names of the heroes from the Greek War of Independence, the fight that freed the country from Ottoman rule. Inside tiny village chapels, I lit beeswax candles and bowed my head under the transcendent gaze of Saint Nicholas, the patron saint of travelers. I spent hours upon hours learning Greek vocabulary. In dance class, I worked to get the steps right, held my handkerchief high, kicked my heels. I bought Greek cigarettes and ate Greek chocolate. At a downtown old-world café called Zonar's, I drank my coffee the Greek way, *metrio*, with sugar. I even wandered down streets wearing long black skirts, as if I was already a *yia-yia*, my husband dead, my children grown. As I did all of these things, I kept score. Every time I fooled someone into thinking I was Greek, I won. Leslie, one point. America, zero.

Shame followed me anyway. Each day it grew bigger.

My hidden wish, for Dad's secret to be revealed, drove me to cafés in leftist neighborhoods, where anti-establishment students smoked endless cigarettes and cut their eyes at the world. I was certain they would realize that I was no ordinary American. I imagined them leaping to their feet and screaming, "Traitor! Daughter of an American spy!"

"It wasn't me! I didn't do it!" I would yell back, but it wouldn't matter.

Nothing I said or did allowed me to outrun my feelings.

***

I made friends with another student in the program. Chris was thin and athletic, a tennis player. Her mother was Greek-American but grew up in the U.S. Still, Chris understood Greek culture the way I did. I told her about Susan, but I didn't say the words *lesbian* or *in love*. I kept all that out of it. What Susan and I had was "intense," I said.

I wrote Susan from Greece, desperate to somehow get "us" back. In my letters, I acted as if we were still friends, as if she hadn't knocked over a mailbox in anger. This was the only way I knew to try and hold onto her.

"How's the food this semester?" I asked.

Her letters back were as superficial as mine. I was sure she still hated me.

For Easter break, I traveled to a small village in the Peloponnesus and rented a room in an old couple's home. They were friendly and served me coffee. They offered me a small room in the back of their house and charged me little. The old woman told me about her daughter who had moved to Athens. I saw the sorrow in her eyes. I nodded as she told me her stories.

I walked the muddy road above the village. Everyone I passed greeted me and asked me where I was from. I told them "Ameriki," and they smiled. They weren't city Greeks who hated the U.S. for setting up the dictatorship; they loved America and told me about their relatives in Chicago or Boston. When they offered to serve me coffee and biscuits, I felt the warmth of my Greece, the one I remembered.

I talked to Dad a few times during the semester. I waited in a long line at the National Telephone Company before stepping into the small booth and placing my call. He asked if I was enjoying Greece and having a good time. I didn't say how mixed up I felt. Instead, I told him safe things—the names of islands I had visited and the foods I had eaten. I mentioned going to a café called Zonar's downtown.

"I used to go there a lot!" he said brightly. "It was a great spot."

At the end of the semester, just before I left, PASOK, the Socialist Party, swept the elections to win a second term. I walked to the center of Athens to witness the celebration. Constitution Square was glutted with people. Students from the university climbed light poles and raised fists. The crowd roared as one. I had never witnessed such political fervor. I swayed inside the mass of people. My body felt weightless. I loved the open passion Greeks had for politics. But it was all about hating America. A huge white banner soared across the square like a giant sail, graceful and wide. I looked up and read its message: "Bases out of Greece! Down with the CIA!" Sour spit filled my mouth. Dad again. His Greece. His past. And just as I had started to feel Greek again. It didn't matter because if people knew the truth, I was sure they would curse me. Anger rose in my throat—for me and for Greece, a country that had suffered through a brutal dictatorship and that suffered from it still. I stumbled out of the throng and leaned against a building on the edge of the square. Sweat drenched my T-shirt. Instead of the exuberant chanting, all I heard was the blood pounding inside my skull. I had come to Greece to find myself, but the only person waiting here was my father.

9. The Truth Does Not Set Me Free

When I got off the plane in Miami, Dad greeted me. He smiled cheerfully and said, "*Kalos orises.*" Welcome back. He said it like he had missed me, like he was proud of me for going abroad. He and Cindy married that summer. They gave me and Evelyn pendants marking the day, and we ate lobster and steak and looked out at the Atlantic Ocean. It was a pleasant event but it didn't lessen my overall depression. Afterward, Dad and Cindy sold their condos and moved to Virginia.

It wasn't until a break that year that I traveled to see their new house. I flew from Boston to Richmond. When Dad picked me up, he said Cindy and Evelyn were already there. I stared at the countryside as Dad navigated the winding roads of Virginia. Eventually, he pulled to a stop at an unassuming cinderblock gatehouse. I didn't see any other buildings around. Where exactly were we?

Dad got out of the car just as a uniformed guard stepped out of the gatehouse. I watched the two of them discuss something. The guard motioned for me to get out of the car, which I did. Somewhere in the distance, popping sounds shattered the air like firecrackers. I looked down the road and thought, *guns*, but said nothing.

The guard motioned for me to enter the small structure. My palms sweat. He lifted a clipboard from his desk and said in a matter-of-fact voice, "This is a CIA base. Everyone who lives here—and their guests—has to sign saying they won't disclose this information to anyone."

The truth vibrated through me. It broke the silence of years inside me. It didn't matter that a total stranger had told me this. Or even that I had been lied to for so long. It just mattered that I had finally learned the truth. Officially. Dad was in the CIA. The fog lifted. My body felt light. I wanted the moment to last forever. But just like the moment in the car with Mom years before, this moment was short-lived.

The guard stood before me, clipboard in hand, waiting for my signature. I pushed my hair out of my eyes, reached for the pen, and signed my name. He then told me to have a seat and took a photo of me for the badge I'd need to show when entering and exiting the base. I stared without expression as the flash went off. I hadn't been freed from Dad's secret. I had been tethered to it. It was mine to carry now, and mine to hide.

Life on the base was dull. All the houses sat far apart, making it difficult for Evelyn and me to meet anyone. At least spending days together brought us closer. Evelyn talked about transferring to an art school in Boston, and I was glad. We would be near each other and back in each other's lives.

In the afternoons, we walked roads that looped back on themselves, going nowhere. Sometimes we heard gunshots in the distance but could never pinpoint their location. We asked each other, "Is Dad shooting those guns?" We didn't know, but we piled our anger onto him anyway. He was the one who had made us move as kids, who only thought about his work, even when Mom was at her sickest. And now she was gone, and we were stuck with him, trapped in his world.

10. Finding My Words

Junior year, in the middle of a winter snowstorm, I ran into Susan on campus. I felt the old impulse to be near her, so I invited her to see my new dorm. Excited, we trudged through snowy streets to my building and took the elevator to the fifth floor. My room was cold. Heavy, wide flakes plummeted onto Beacon Street. Susan sat on my bed with that same expectant gaze, the one that wanted to know who I was and what I wanted.

She didn't wait hours this time. "You still don't know what you want, do you?"

"I want us to be friends," I said, still engulfed in confusion. How could other people, Susan included, always be so sure?

"What the fuck does that mean?" she said.

She got up and stormed out of the room. It was a replay of our previous argument, and I couldn't blame her. Only myself.

***

In one of my sociology classes, I made friends with two gay boys. We talked about sexism, and I told them I was looking for a feminist man. They laughed and said, "That's what we are, honey, but we're not available." We went to gay bars on Friday nights. The windows were painted black, and disco-y music pumped on all three floors. Straight and gay people sat around small tables. I told myself that's what I was doing too—hanging out with my gay friends. We ordered gin and tonics, danced, and boy-watched together. When they invited me to go with them to Gay Pride, I said yes. I told myself I was their straight friend. I walked the narrow downtown streets of Boston's Back Bay neighborhood in my first-ever Gay Pride parade. Not out. Not sure of who or what I was. I convinced myself that as long as I kept moving my identity from one place to another, I could avoid facing whoever it is I actually was.

***

I told Linda about my confusion. She said therapy might help me sort things out, so I found a feminist therapy collective in Somerville, a working-class suburb of Boston. I called and set up an appointment. On the day of my first session, I rode the city bus a half hour to a small Victorian house with gray and blue painted trim where I sat in a room and cried. That was all I did. Cry. The therapist assigned to me had short, curly, salt-and-pepper hair. She asked me what was making me cry. I said I didn't know. But the truth was that everything was making me cry. I didn't know how to parse it all out. She asked the same question the following week and the week after that. How could I find words for things that had been wordless for years? I wanted my therapist to give me her words, but she wouldn't. She just sat and waited for me to find my own.

"It's all a jumble," I said in my third session.

"What is?"

"My life."

I told her that my mother had died, and more recently, my grandmother Janet. I told her my father was always away working. I used rudimentary terms. I said he was in the CIA and that this forced us to move often. I dissolved into tears again.

"Why do I cry so much?"

She said there was a scale that measured the impact of traumatic events. The death of a parent was number one. Moving was also high on the list.

"You have plenty of reasons to cry," she said.

She said keeping a journal might help me locate and express what I felt, so I went to the local feminist bookstore and found one with an image of a woman dreaming on the cover. I didn't know how this would help or if it could, but I bought it anyway. Each time I sat down to write, I told myself that no one would read what I had written. I wrote uncensored. My hand tried to keep up as anger and sorrow raced each other across the page. I wrote the words *Dad never gives me what I need* over and over again. Each journal entry brought more of my anger to the surface. I was sure he was to blame, if not for everything, for so much—Mom's death, my loneliness, my inability to know myself, all my sadness. He was responsible for world events too. His work in the CIA played a role in things one way or another.

In 1986, the Iran-Contra scandal broke, and the world learned that officials from the Reagan administration had secretly facilitated the sale of arms to Iran in order to fund a war in Nicaragua. The proceeds of the arms sales were sent to fund the Contras in their effort to overturn Nicaragua's socialist government. I thought, *American imperialism did this. Dad did this.*

I brought up the scandal in a phone call with him, nervously winding and unwinding the tight spiral phone cord as we talked. I said the CIA had sold guns illegally to Iran to fund the war in Central America. Dad asked where I had gotten this information. He acted as if I had been babbling some fringe conspiracy theory.

"The *Miami Herald*," I said.

"The *Herald* doesn't print the truth." The calmness in his voice meant I couldn't possibly know what I was talking about. It was a familiar feeling.

I brought up the name of the CIA officer accused of selling guns. I stammered as I talked. Whatever I said, Dad's voice stayed even and calm.

Eventually, I lost it. "He was corrupt! He sold drugs for money!"

"Did that come from the *Herald* too?" Dad asked.

It was as if I'd gone completely off the rails, as if believing an article in a major U.S. newspaper made me crazy.

"So, there's never been a corrupt CIA officer in the whole history of the CIA? Not one bad apple?" I was losing the argument, even though I had read it in the paper.

"That's right," Dad said.

I rolled my eyes.

Fine, I thought after we hung up. *You can have your perfect and flawless version of America, and I'll have mine.*

***

Graduation day arrived with all the trappings of a picture-perfect family, except that most of the family was missing. Grandmother Janet had died a few years before, and Mom was gone, of course. Ole G.A. came. I hadn't seen her in a few years. It felt strange to see her outside of San Antonio. Tom and Linda arrived too—my uncle in his tweed professor's jacket and Linda in her suffragette bun and long wool coat. Evelyn was there, looking like she was as excited by "family time" as I was. After the ceremony, we made our way to an Italian restaurant for dinner. Dad and Cindy sat together at the far end of the table. I wanted to be happy, but it didn't really feel like we were together. It was more like we were disparate factions that had met briefly for a common purpose.

I moved out of the dorms and into a three-bedroom apartment with new roommates. A month later, I got a job running a food pantry inside the women's center at Boston City Hospital. Every morning, I gave out neon-orange, Reagan-era cheese blocks and boxes of powdered milk to women younger than me. They watched me hustle around the supply room for food I didn't need and had never tried.

After work, I bumped into someone I knew from the dorms. A boy.

He invited me over to his apartment, where we sat on floor cushions, talked, and ate rice from small bowls. After dinner, we went to his bedroom. There was no light as we took off our clothes. *I'll try this*, I told myself. We said nothing as we had quick, mechanical sex. He got up to shower afterward while I lay in bed with no orgasm and no warmth.

I told my therapist that I had slept with a boy in our next session and that it was nothing special. I told her about Susan too. I used the phrase "in love." I told her that what I felt with Susan was exciting, even though nothing had ever happened sexually.

"Does that make me gay?" I asked. Associating the word with me, and not someone else, felt awkward, like walking backward. Or swimming in something not meant for swimming, oil or glue. I waited for her answer, certain she'd know.

"What do you think?" she said.

I hated this way she had of always waiting for me to lead.

"Maybe," I heard myself say. "Or maybe I'm bi."

Later, I scribbled the word *bisexual* into my journal.

It felt right, both the way it sat on the page and within me.

11. Fucking CIA

I arrived at the gay bar in Boston's Fenway neighborhood wearing a black leather motorcycle jacket and Doc Marten boots. I grabbed a table to wait for Chris, my friend from Greece who was now a tennis pro. We'd been flirting over the phone for months. She had graduated too, and was living with her parents on the north shore. I spotted her coming down the stairs in a blindingly white tennis skirt. Everyone else wore black like me.

"I thought embarrassing you would be a good move," she said, smiling.

We'd been talking about going out for months. And now we were.

We ordered White Russians, drained them fast, and hit the dance floor. The house music pulsed. I tried to loosen up and move from friendship mode to something else. A slow song came up. I turned to leave the dance floor, but Chris caught my hand and pulled me toward her. Our bodies pressed together, and just like that, in a single moment, everything changed. We held each other, swayed to the music, and kissed. It felt natural. All the years of hiding fell away. *This is me*, I thought. *This is who I am.*

***

I might have been ready to be myself with Chris, but I wasn't ready to tell others. Especially not Dad. When he and Cindy invited me and Evelyn to New York City for Christmas months later, I wavered about telling them. In the afternoons, we walked up and down Fifth Avenue in the freezing wind while we window-shopped. I told them about my new job working as a caseworker for the elderly but said nothing about my personal life. One evening, we ducked inside a midtown eatery. Fluorescent lights illuminated greasy buffet food, and holiday music tinkled from overhead speakers. We filled our trays with plates of macaroni and cheese and chicken wings and found a corner booth. As soon as we sat down, Cindy gave me and Evelyn a sympathetic look.

"Your father has something he wants to say to you girls."

I shifted in my chair. I didn't like where things seemed to be going.

Dad looked stiff and bulky in his coat, his red plaid scarf still wrapped around his neck. "I should have taken you all with me when I was stationed in Vietnam. You would have lived on an Army base in the Philippines, but then maybe your mother wouldn't have had such a hard time in San Antonio."

He was talking about Mom's breakdown. I felt blindsided. We had never talked about this before. I looked over at Cindy huddled inside her winter coat. This was her idea.

"Course that would have been tough," Dad continued. "Bases aren't very uplifting." He said Mom wouldn't have known anyone in the Philippines, "But at least I would have been around more. Your mother and I both thought she would be better off in San Antonio with family. Turns out that was a bad plan. Maybe if I had moved you to the Philippines, your mother wouldn't have been hospitalized the way she was."

Tears streamed down Dad's face.

I wanted to be the kind of daughter who reached across the table and forgave, but I couldn't. Moving to the Philippines wouldn't have saved Mom. Her unhappiness wasn't just about one single move or separation. It was about all the secrets. It was about wanting more out of life. She was the kind of person who poured gallons of paint onto canvases spread across the garage floor and read books like *The Joy of Sex*. She had tried to teach me to listen to myself. And now she was gone. I wanted Dad to feel bad, to know something of what it had been like for me—for all of us—all these years. "Santa Claus Is Coming to Town" droned in the background. The door to the diner swung open, letting in a big gust of cold. Evelyn and I stared silently at the crumbs on our trays until, eventually, Dad and Cindy decided it was time to go, and we left.

***

When I got back to Boston, I thought about Mom, about the divorce she had talked about, the cancer she strained to beat. The life she didn't have the chance to live. But I did; I had the chance. I threw myself into a super-gay, super-feminist life. I attended Pride marches and joined a feminist radio collective that broadcasted a weekly women's news show. I interviewed authors and activists, and the other women in the collective became my sisters. When I came out to them, they congratulated me. I felt almost liberated and almost free. When one of my sisters hosted a show about the CIA-assisted coup in Chile, I didn't tell her she was talking about my father. I also didn't disagree.

At an indoor soccer game, I met a lesbian couple from Cyprus. We became fast friends. I drank in their Greekness like water from a spring—like a memory of myself. I told them I had lived in Greece as a kid and had studied there in college. They invited me over to their apartment and served me slices of salty *Halloumi* with cut tomatoes. Meeting them was like finding a piece of home. It was what I had hoped to find during my college semester in Athens. They made me mixtapes of Greek blues and new wave singers. "You dance like a real Greek," they said, laughing. We sat and talked for hours. They told me the story of how they had met in high school and then both found their way to study in the

United States. "No one is out in Cyprus," Daphne said as her dark eyes flashed. "Women have to meet in back rooms." They told me how they started seeing each other, about what the early days of their relationship had been like. I admired their closeness, the energy between them. I wanted that for myself. A love like that.

It felt like we were under a wide plane tree in a Greek *plateia*. We talked about politics too.

"The U.S. is always overthrowing democracies," Efi said, her accent stronger than Daphne's.

"Not the U.S. generically," Daphne interrupted, correcting her. "The CIA. They do this."

The CIA. The word sunk me like a load of bricks. I wanted to be honest with them. They had shared so much with me. But what would happen if I told them the truth? My heart stormed inside my chest.

"My dad is in the CIA," I said.

They stared at me, shocked or just surprised, I couldn't tell which. A second later, in characteristic roll-with-the-punches Greek style, they shrugged.

"It's not like *you're* in the CIA," Efi said.

Then they told me the story of how Cyprus came to be a divided island—Turkey occupying one-third in the north, and Greek Cypriots controlling the rest. Their words were an avalanche of sorrow.

They said it had been the Greek military's obsessive dream to join Cyprus with Greece and how in 1974, the military junta made its move. They sent their forces to the island to overthrow the Cypriot government, but when they did, Turkey invaded. Days later, the island stood partitioned with Greek Cypriots controlling the south and Turkey occupying part of the north. Barbed wire separated the island.

Daphne said that people had to leave their homes in an instant. Her mother had suitcases ready in case their family had to flee. She glanced around the café and lowered her voice. "The

CIA knew the Greek junta was planning a coup in Cyprus. They knew and did nothing to stop it."

I was numb. I couldn't feel the wooden chair beneath me or the surface of the table beneath my arm. He did this. Dad did this to Cyprus. "Fucking CIA," I said.

I adopted their worldview after that. I wanted to be Greek or Cypriot or both. I thought that if I adopted their views, the views of the locals—those who believed the CIA was behind every bad thing that had happened in Greece and in Cyprus—I would be loved and accepted by them. I would find my place in the world.

***

Not long after my talk with Daphne and Efi, Dad called. He said the agency planned to give him an award for his service. I didn't know what to say. I wasn't ready for this. He wanted to know if I would come to the acceptance ceremony. How could I support wars or clandestine coups or the other horrible things the CIA did? I didn't. I wouldn't. But I felt like a traitor too. What kind of daughter says no to an award ceremony for her father?

On the appointed day, Evelyn and I flew to D.C. Dad and Cindy picked us up from the airport and drove us toward CIA headquarters in Virginia. Once there, we parked and followed Dad into Langley. We passed through security, took an elevator, and walked down a hallway of closed doors. Dad stopped in front of an unmarked door and opened it.

We stepped into a small, wood-paneled room. Thirty or so people filled the room. There were a few faces I recognized, agency families I had known growing up, but most were strangers.

Dad guided us to a middle row and took a seat at the end. Cindy sat next to him, then me, then Evelyn. I was dressed in a vintage, black-and-white 1950s sweater and a long, brown denim skirt. The beveled, silver bracelet Chris (who I was still seeing) had given me hung from my wrist. I scanned the small, nondescript room. A portrait of former CIA director and President George H. W. Bush hung on the far wall next to a 1960s-style clock, its silver hands and numbers affixed directly onto the paneled wall. Unhappy faces of former agency directors lined the other walls. There were no windows and no decorations of any kind.

A man stepped up to the podium and began to speak.

"We are here to honor Michael Absher's service to the United States of America."

I leaned forward, eager to learn something about Dad and his secret work. The man continued to talk, but all he shared were general platitudes. He said Dad was being recognized for his work during the 1980s. I thought about the invasion of Grenada. When the short introduction was over, Dad rose from his chair. People turned around in their seats and watched him approach the front of the room. He stood at the podium in a three-piece, navy blue pinstripe suit. He looked down at the award and then out at the rest of us.

His eyes were soft. "I want to thank everyone for coming today."

He said a few other things, about it not being an easy job, about being proud of the work he and other agency personnel had done. He looked like he wanted to say more but stopped himself. He picked up the small, wooden plaque and started back for our row. I couldn't believe it was over. He had the opportunity to say something about his mystery job, about the secret we had all carried for years, but he didn't share much of anything. He didn't even brag.

People came up to shake hands and congratulate him afterward. A photographer approached and lined us up below the clock. Evelyn stood next to Dad, and I took my place beside Cindy. Once we were in position, Cindy lifted the certificate that accompanied Dad's award so that it would be the focus of the shot. I looked down and read the words "Intelligence Medal of Merit" next to Dad's name. It hit me then. This wasn't an average award. It was a big deal. Who knew what Dad had done to earn it? I clasped my hands in front of me and smiled tightly.

12. DMSG

Dad kept his secrets to himself, and so did I. Just like him, I lived a double life. One life had my queer self in it, and the other didn't. It wasn't strange to go back and forth—to tell some secrets but not others. It felt old. Easy. At least Evelyn accepted me. When I told her I was going to the Pride Parade, by way of coming out to her, she said, "Have fun!" And Pride was fun, but it didn't take away my loneliness. I wrote pages and pages about love and longing in my journal. I wrote about wishing I was in love with Chris and another girl I was seeing, the way I had once felt for Susan. *Susan.* I stared at her name on the page. I tore a sheet from my journal and wrote a letter.

"I was in love with you," I said. "You're probably still a Republican and super-closeted, but I just wanted you to know that I'm gay. A part of me is always looking for you and what we had." I asked my college roommate, Gail, who was still in touch with Susan, for her address. I held my breath as I folded the page around a cassette of Tracy Chapman's *Revolution* and mailed it off.

Two weeks later, I got Susan's reply.

She was glad I had finally figured it out, she said, and told me she wasn't closeted. She said she had dealt with her sexuality a long time ago. "It's interesting, you dusting off these old memories, but I choose to leave them where they are." It was her last line that hurt the most: "I would prefer it if you never contact me again."

Fine, I thought, pulling out a book of matches, striking one and touching the flame to the corner of her letter. *I won't.*

***

I tried to reframe romance and love after that. It seemed like the only way to lessen my hurt over Susan's rejection. I told myself that "being in love" didn't actually exist. It was just a concept rooted in oppression. I wouldn't live according to the patriarchy's norms. Instead, I would live according to my own.

I got a second part-time job tutoring at a community college, but when my two jobs didn't pay enough for me to support myself, I called Linda for advice. I hadn't seen her since she and my uncle had gotten divorced. We weren't in touch as much as we used to be, but I still needed her. She said I should consider getting another degree. She said Harvard had a master's in education with leading feminist scholars. I sent in my application along with an essay about wanting to help build grassroots women's communities. Months later, I received an acceptance letter.

I arrived on campus and signed up for a class on the development of girls and women taught by a protégé of feminist scholar, Carol Gilligan. After the first lecture, I struck up a conversation with two women who had lost their mothers when they were young. We formed a group called the Dead Mothers Support Group, or DMSG for short. A touch of the macabre in the name was okay with us. Losing our moms when we were kids was traumatic. Why sugarcoat it? After every class, we swapped stories and cried. A woman in her fifties said to me, "You're lucky you're talking about losing your mom now. It took me years to open up." She seemed to admire me, but I wasn't sure why. I was talking about losing my mom with her and the other women because I didn't think the grief would ever stop. Still, I wanted it to.

I asked my therapist if my mother-loss grief would ever go away. She sat quietly in her chair, watching me. I wanted her to save me from my tears and tell me there would be an end to it one day, but she didn't. Some days, grief kept me from leaving my apartment.

At the end of the year, when I finished my degree, Dad, Cindy, and Evelyn came to my graduation ceremony. We sat in a café sipping iced tea and trying to make small talk. At some point, Dad admitted he'd never really liked Boston. He didn't say it, but I knew he thought Boston was too liberal and too homosexual, which was fine with me because the South, where he lived, was all kinds of wrong for me.

***

After graduation, I filled out an endless stream of job applications before landing one teaching high school dropouts. I wasn't prepared for how difficult it would be. They seemed sad, like me, but their lives were harder—battling poverty and institutionalized racism. Their struggles overwhelmed me. I didn't know how to help them. My only strategy was to fake it— just like I had done while working for Delta Airlines. I didn't feel prepared for any job. Each morning, I ignored my racing pulse and went to the job anyway. When I arrived, I told my students to open their journals and try expressing their feelings. I pretended it didn't hurt when they said, "This is stupid." They dropped their heads onto their desks and slept. Some days I spent my lunch break in the bathroom crying. Was it grief over losing my mother? All of the moving I experienced as a kid?

Next door to the GED program was a yoga center. It was a struggle to follow all the directions at first: push sitting bones toward the ceiling, grip the floor with all five toes. My muscles stretched and relaxed. In each class, I went inside myself and focused on my breath. I didn't have to fake anything because it wasn't about the outside world. I could be whoever and however I wanted. At the end of class, we did what the teacher described as the hardest pose, the *Savasana*-corpse. We lay in the darkened room, eyes closed, faces upturned toward the sky beyond the roof. Thoughts skidded into shapelessness, and my breath slowed as tears slid from my eyes, crossed my temples, and pooled inside my ears.

I heard a voice. *Be who you are*, it said.

I sat down at my kitchen table and composed another letter, this time to my father. I had absorbed lessons from feminism and gay rights—being free meant letting go of old fears. It was time to come out where it mattered most. I formed the words that would finally tell Dad who I was. "I'm gay," I wrote. I was terrified to become visible after so many years of not sharing anything real about my life. It felt like a blow to the chest, all my breath pushed out. Still, I finished my letter and sent it off.

Dad called the day he received it. "I can't accept this. It's not natural," he said.

I felt sweaty and sick.

"But there's no reason for us to lose contact," he added.

When we hung up, my sexuality sat between us, disclosed but not accepted.

"How can he say that?" I told my therapist later.

"Have you ever thought that maybe he can't give you what you want?" she answered.

It didn't make sense to go back into the closet with Dad, but that's exactly what I did. I stopped telling him anything important or personal. We were used to closing things off. I tried to not expect anything. Whenever I slipped up or chanced a sliver of sharing, like telling him I was tired of teaching GED and wanted a job that didn't burn me out, he said, "How about a job with the military?" or "Why don't you move to the Sunbelt? There are lots of jobs there!" He didn't get me, and never would. We talked less and less after that, until the distance between us started to feel complete.

13. Political Correctness

Dad and I grew more and more apart. I convinced myself this was how it had to be. We would never be close; we were just too different. Over time, I would have to get used to not having a father. I couldn't admit how much I was hurting and how much I still needed both of my parents.

Then one morning, Cindy called.

"Have you heard?" she asked. Her voice was high-pitched and frantic.

She said a gunman had lain in wait outside CIA headquarters during morning rush hour traffic. While motorists sat at a standstill at the turnoff to CIA headquarters, the gunman got out of his car and began walking up and down the line of cars shooting through car windows with an AK-47 assault rifle. Two agency employees had been killed. The day was January 25, 1993.

"Dad was just ten minutes away," Cindy said. "It could have been your father!"

"He's okay, right?" I said, trying to steady her.

But it was me who needed steadying. I sat down on the edge of my futon, my mind spinning. I didn't feel the distance between us. Instead, I felt the connection. The father who had always pulsed at the edge of my life, the one I told myself to stop needing, was almost taken from me. It could have happened. He could be gone now. Not just Mom but Dad too. My chest shook. The sobs seemed to come out of nowhere.

I must have called him later that day. I would have said how relieved I was that he was safe and that he had arrived ten minutes late. I know I would have done this, but I don't remember the details—the words I used or how he responded. I don't remember if he acknowledged his vulnerability or only expressed anger at the gunman. I don't remember his response.

But I do remember his call six months later. And my reaction.

"After nearly thirty-two years with the agency, I've decided to retire."

"What?" I asked, not following.

"I'm retiring," he said. "I want to teach."

His voice sounded lighter than usual.

"Teach what?" I asked, still trying to catch up with the news.

"Intelligence."

I tried to process this. I couldn't imagine him not being a spy, just like I couldn't imagine him getting a job where he talked about having been one.

He explained that in order to teach, the agency would enact the process of removing his covers. It would review all the places he had worked undercover. It would also review his former and current contacts to see if disclosing his identity as a former agency official would put him or anyone else in danger. It felt extra real, but at the same time, farfetched. He sounded upbeat, like it was something he was actually looking forward to. I didn't feel ready for any of it. All my life he had hidden his identity. How could he change now? Who would he become? Who would I?

***

Dad's enthusiasm didn't last long.

A few weeks into his first teaching gig at the University of Texas in San Antonio, Cindy called. Her voice sounded ragged. "Your father won't tell you what's really happening, but some people don't want him there and they protest his class, which is their right, of course, but he gets 'notes,' Leslie, and they aren't nice notes."

"Political correctness," Dad groused when Cindy handed him the phone. "The CIA is bad, blah, blah, blah."

I tried to imagine what was happening. I pictured students demonstrating against Dad's presence on campus, against CIA covert actions the world over. I imagined that they were like me— liberal and opposed to U.S. imperialism. *It's good for him to know what people think about the CIA*, I thought smugly, pretending not to hear the part about the notes.

***

That summer, I stood on a backyard deck at a friend's party, sipping beer with a girl from my soccer team. The team was like a lesbian tribe, my de-facto family. We hung out after games and on weekends and talked about our childhoods. Mainstream society dictated the nuclear family as central. For me, it was my tribe of friends that held me up in this world.

Sharon's curly blonde hair framed her full face. I told her my theory about romantic love being a false ideal. She agreed but said that there were lots of ways to feel romantic. Sharon had gone to Oberlin. She was more evolved than me.

The following week, we went for dinner at an upscale restaurant. Sharon wore a pretty dress and shoes that were almost heels.

"Look at you," I said.

Sharon blushed. "You like?"

My eyes said yes.

We started dating. I could talk to her about anything. I told her I loved her, which was true even if I wasn't *in love* with her.

***

That summer, Daphne and Efi and I drifted apart. The friendship that once made me feel at home ended. It had been five years since my college semester in Greece. Losing my friendship with them made me miss it more. I planned a vacation in early June. I would fly to Athens and then go straight to Skopelos, one of the greenest islands in the Aegean, via bus and ferry. My own Greek odyssey.

I arrived, found a room, and set out on a walk above the port town.

I greeted people as I walked. When a man asked about my accent and where I had learned to speak Greek so well, I said I had lived in Athens when I was small.

"My father was a businessman," I said.

"Ah," he said approvingly.

One day, I passed an old woman dressed in mourner's clothing on her balcony.

"Come!" she said, beckoning me up to her tiny apartment.

I took a seat at her table and watched as she cut squash blossoms from their stems. One by one, she lined her counter with orange-colored blossoms. She stuffed each with cheese, doused them with salt, and carefully turned them inside a bowl of flour. She fried them in a skillet, then placed them on a paper towel, brushed her hands onto her apron, and brought over a plate piled high with fried flowers, limp and oily. I took one and bit into it. I let the tang of Greece melt in my mouth. For the first time in so long, I was exactly where I was meant to be.

14. Glenwood Road

The feeling I had on Skopelos made me want to create a home in Boston too. After Evelyn graduated from art school and broke up with her long-term boyfriend, I decided to buy a house. I wanted to create a home for the two of us, one we would never have to leave. I called Dad and asked about the trust fund Grandfather had left me after he died. Dad hadn't kept me updated about the account. That rankled me; it seemed like yet another secret. I asked him how much was in the account. He was cagey at first, but I kept pressing.

"Fifty thousand," he said eventually.

It was more than enough for a down payment.

I found a three-story place on a working-class street in the middle of Somerville that needed a lot of work. Evelyn moved into the third floor, an attic space with its own side entrance. I took the second floor, and the family that was already renting on the first floor stayed. Evelyn and I worked side by side. We laughed at the orange seventies shag carpet and retro wood paneling as we tore both out. I felt the hum of having my sister beside me again. We looked at the warped walls underneath—at all the cracks and dips—and shook our heads. Evelyn was precise with measurements and tools. She created a kitchenette for her attic apartment and retiled its small bathroom. We had made homes for ourselves—for a while.

When Dad and Cindy invited us to New York City for Christmas again, I thought, *This never works out.* I went anyway, tucking my first published story, a prose poem about Mom, into my Army green messenger bag.

The second night after arriving, we went to the opera. Afterward, the four of us made our way to a diner, put our names on the waiting list, and stood outside. I reached into my canvas bag and pulled out the *Berkeley Fiction Review*, a journal that had published one of my prose poems. The frigid wind whipped my cheeks.

"I had something published," I said. "It's about Mom."

People pushed into me, trying to get by. Dad seemed distracted. He was grayer now than he used to be but still as energetic as always. He kept his eye on the hostess. I could tell he thought she was letting other customers get ahead of us. I handed him the journal, the page open to my prose poem, *Swallowing My Mother*:

> When I swallowed my mother, I swallowed her thick dark hair and smooth teeth. I swallowed her tapered legs and tiny wrists...But when I swallowed my mother, I saw how I had also swallowed her scolding. 'Hold your shoulders back. Sit up straight.' Her standards of behavior...And with the scolding, I swallowed her carefully appraising eye...The one that follows me around at parties, pitting people against each other, against me, against those I love...Now it is all mine. The eye that looks out and in with the power to see everything ugly or deeply beautiful.

I longed to take back the journal as I watched him read, but it was too late. Why was I risking myself with him yet again? My therapist said I kept looking for things he couldn't give me. Here I was doing it again. I didn't understand the impulse within me to reach out. Or why I kept doing it even when it didn't work, when I experienced only disappointment. Instead of seeing it for what it was, something good that could lead me to feel closer one day, I kept trying to circumvent it, stifling my own nature.

He handed the book back to me. "It's interesting how you see your mother."

The moment felt familiar. My impulse to show him who I was, to open up and not stay closed, the gamble of it, had backfired once again. He didn't get me or Mom's complex impact on my life. She had been someone who had taught me to break silences, which had led to me writing this poem and getting it published. But she had also taught me to focus on my appearance. Dad didn't seem to get this mixed legacy. I jammed the journal back into my messenger bag as the hostess called his name, and we made our way into the loud, packed diner.

***

I went back to my usual stance with Dad. Whenever we spoke by phone, I shared as little as possible. He didn't push beyond small talk either. One day, he called to say he'd be driving through Boston on his way to a high school reunion in New Hampshire and asked if I wanted to meet him somewhere along the way. It was the same drama again, I was sure. It wouldn't work out. Our recent NYC trip had proven that. Except that this time, Dad had been the one to reach out.

We arranged to meet at a local Cambridge café. Before we hung up, I mentioned that I might bring a friend or two, people I'd like him to meet. I didn't say "girlfriend" or "lover." I thought about inviting Evelyn, but we had started to argue about the house and the amount of rent she paid. I offered to lower it, but this didn't seem to make a difference. She began to come and go from her separate entrance without saying hello.

On the appointed day of my meeting with Dad, with Sharon and my friends already at the café, I stopped just blocks away at a phone booth. My body felt heavy with dread. He was an expert at disappearing acts. I dialed in for my messages and heard one from him.

His voice deflated me. "I can't make it today."

Days later, after the reunion had ended, he called. Maybe he heard the hurt in my voice. He offered to reschedule our visit, and so I scrambled to reassemble everyone—this time, around the New England farm table in my kitchen. I knew it probably wouldn't end well, but the impulse to try was something I couldn't stop. I hoped anyway.

When Dad and Cindy arrived at my doorstep, I led them upstairs to the kitchen. Dad seemed surprised to find that it wasn't just me, that I'd assembled my whole lesbian tribe. He looked awkward meeting a group of strangers, but I had to—how else would he know me if he didn't meet people who were important to me? I introduced Sharon, calling her a "friend," and wishing I had the courage to say she was my girlfriend. Sharon took it in stride.

It wasn't a perfect gathering but at least it had happened. I could tell how uncomfortable it made Dad. He hunched inside his navy-blue suit jacket as if it were necessary armor. My friends chatted amiably. When I spoke, he looked bewildered and squinted as if the room were filled with smoke.

15. Her Face Round Like the Moon

I was finding my way at work and in life. Sort of. But I couldn't seem to find the love I longed for. The powerful kind I had witnessed between Daphne and Efi—and once felt for Susan. Then one day, inside my journal, something definitive and clear landed on the page: If only Susan and I had become lovers, I would have the answers to my questions.

I stared at the simple sentence.

A week later, on a Thursday night, Gail, my roommate from college, called.

"Where are you?" I asked. I could hardly hear her voice above the din.

"At the Hideaway," Gail said.

"That dyke pool place?"

"Yes." Gail said I should come out and meet them. When I asked who she was talking about, she said, "Me and Susan."

"Susan who?"

"*Susan* Susan," Gail said. She said Susan had given her the change to call me.

A flame of heat climbed my neck as I jumped into my faded red Toyota Corona with the Uppity Women Unite bumper sticker and drove through Somerville's back streets to the Hideaway's gravel-strewn parking lot. Inside, women in their late twenties and early thirties milled around the short bar. I scanned the room until I saw her. My legs wobbled. Susan looked professional in a white dress shirt and black slacks, her medium-brown hair shoulder length.

"Hey," I said, arriving at the end of the bar where she and Gail sipped beers.

"Hey," Susan said back.

When I asked what they were drinking, Susan turned the bottle around to read the label and said, "What am I having, Gail?"

Gail giggled.

I laughed, too, and ordered a White Russian from a bartender in a sleeveless muscle shirt pulling beers. We found a booth and sat down. I tried to adjust to the fact that Susan was sitting across from me for the first time in eleven years. For so long, she'd been a memory, and now she was here.

"I burned that letter you sent me," I said.

Susan smiled. "I burned yours too."

"I also called you once and hung up," I confessed. "It was the middle of the night, but it was worth it to hear your voice."

"That was you? You were stalking me?" Susan looked pleased.

We decided to play pool. Susan slid quarters into the table, and I lined up the balls. The three of us joked as we played. My face heated up as I leaned over the green felt surface for a shot. After a few games, we left for my place. Gail fell asleep on the futon sofa, while Susan and I talked as if we were eighteen again. This time our words flowed without stopping. Susan said she and her last girlfriend had broken up a few years ago. I told her about Sharon. Susan nodded. Already, I felt like I was cheating.

"What made you want to get in touch?" I asked.

"You've been this ghost in my life for years. I wanted to see you, let you go and move on."

I tried to chart the color of Susan's eyes. They were blue but not ordinary blue. More like bottom-of-a-swimming-pool blue, at night, with all the lights turned on. We talked about everything—how my depression made me turn away from her, how long it had taken me to find myself, to start healing from my mother's death, and how I couldn't have done any of it without my therapist.

"I'm sorry I hurt you," I said, tears welling up. I was grateful to feel them and to see the easy way Susan accepted my apology.

"I'm sorry too," she said, "for sending my letter."

We sat quietly inside the huge miracle of the moment. When pinks and yellows started to light up the sky, Susan said she had to pick up a friend at the airport and drive to a memorial service in Maine. She said that maybe she could stop by again before she flew back to California.

Two days later, she was back on my futon sofa.

"Your eyes are like smoky topaz," she said.

The slate rooftops of Somerville crowded behind her through the bay window. She was all I had thought about. I tried to hold back my smile and act casual, but I couldn't. I felt mute. Time passed. It grew late. I told her she didn't have to leave. She could sleep on the futon sofa. I left the room to search for clean sheets, thinking, *What am I doing? I have a girlfriend.* I returned and found Susan with a wry look on her face. I panicked. She hadn't pulled out the futon yet.

"I forgot a pillow," I said, retreating to my room. I paced the floorboards. *I can't let her go again*, I thought. All I wanted to do was tell her I loved her.

I came back to the living room. "Why don't you sleep in my bed? We can hold each other and be sweet." I had no idea what I meant exactly, but I felt an urgency I couldn't explain.

We lay side by side and gave each other tentative kisses. My head rested below hers, and when she closed her eyes, I studied her face. It was beautiful and strange to see her from this angle, her cheeks a wide plane, her face round like the moon.

In the morning, I dressed for work, pulling on black jeans and a boxy, patterned dress shirt. Susan watched from the bed. While I was in the bathroom, she dressed and called a cab for the airport. We went downstairs. Susan dragged her suitcase behind her, and we said goodbye on the front porch. I felt my life shift. Who was this person I was in love with again? Was she the same Republican she once was? I placed my hand on her cheek, and we kissed. I couldn't have stopped any of it. Nor did I want to.

***

Susan sent me letters from California, from the desk at the big law firm where she worked—yellow legal pad pages filled front to back with her Declaration of Independence handwriting. I stood on the rust-colored pine floors where I did yoga and read each letter over and over again. "I want to grow old with you," she wrote. "I imagine us in our eighties, making love."

"You can't write those things to me," I said later over the phone.

"Why not?"

"I have a girlfriend. I don't know what I'm doing. What we're doing."

At night, I put on Prince and danced around in my shiny orange bra, crazed, unleashed. I was a woman possessed; something was inside me, and I felt outside of myself.

***

A month later, I bought a ticket to California to see what this was. Maybe once I saw her again, this feeling would disappear, and I could continue with my life as I knew it—the steady life I'd made. *Maybe it's infatuation*, I thought.

Before I traveled, I tried to explain to Sharon that we weren't breaking up, that I was just confused. She knew about Susan from my college days. I reassured Sharon that we were still strong. "I just need to sort things out inside myself," I said. She nodded. Her light blue eyes seemed uncertain, but she let me go.

Fear hit me as I made my way down the ramp into the San Francisco airport terminal, as if at the end of the ramp there would be no airport building, just the wide Pacific Ocean, and I'd drop into its waves and sink and be lost.

Susan was there, all curling hair and open smile.

"It's you again," I said.

We stepped onto the escalator. My legs felt unreliable. Light flooded the terminal from a nearby bank of windows. Susan offered to take my bag, but I told her I had it. I needed something to hold onto.

"We have reservations at a jazz sushi club tonight," she said.

Had I told her I loved sushi and jazz?

Minutes later, in Susan's Explorer, guilt flooded me. *What am I doing to me and Sharon?* I wanted to be a good person, but I also wanted Susan. My fingertips lightly stroked Susan's forearm as she drove.

"You're going to make me swerve off the road," she said. That smile.

"Why do you have an Explorer?" I asked. "They're gas guzzlers. Think about the environment."

Her smile widened.

The house she took me to—her house—was a cabin in the trees. When she said her roommate was away for the weekend, my cheeks flushed. She took me downstairs and opened the door to her bedroom. A kind of love-terror seized me when I saw an enormous vase with Birds of Paradise, giant exploding purple dahlias, and yellow roses.

"Those are for you," she said.

But I didn't want them to be for me because it was too much and I was losing my grip.

I saw her bed nestled into the far corner, sumptuously covered with a plush green comforter and wine-colored pillows.

"I need to go upstairs," I stammered.

On the living room sofa, Susan leaned in, and we kissed. Our kisses were openmouthed, round and deep. They went on and on. We tumbled and danced, melted and collided into each other. My heart pounded, and I started to pant. My body wanted more and more, wanted it all.

***

It took a month to break up with Sharon, and nearly a year to leave work, say goodbye to friends, and pack my things. I told Evelyn I was moving but assured her that I wasn't selling my house. "You can stay," I said. When it was time to say goodbye, we hugged stiffly. I didn't know what to do about the space between us, the distance that grew wider every day. Instead, I focused on my new future.

I told Dad too, said I had met a woman and was moving to California. I wanted to get off the phone as quickly as possible. He didn't say much. He seemed to hear the "moving" part but not the "lesbian" part. As if I was moving because I had gotten a job offer. I told myself what I always did—that he and I were too different, that he would never understand me. Defiance had become a kind of coping skill by then. A worn groove within me.

***

When I arrived in California, I breathed in its dry green scent as I sat on Susan's deck, a new journal open in my lap. The questions I'd scribbled for years disappeared. I stopped writing about sadness and loneliness and romantic love being an illusion. Instead, I wrote about finding the person I'd been looking for always. Blank pages filled with gratitude.

In Susan's house—our house—there were only shared rooms. Susan told me I could turn the garage (separated from the house by a set of stairs) into a place to write. We disconnected the garage door and lay down a beige carpet over raw wood floorboards. The ceiling stayed bare and unfinished, with two-by-fours holding up a plywood roof. She helped me carry my old New England farm table up the external stairs into the garage-turned-writing space. It wasn't fancy or finished, but it was mine.

There was nothing about California that didn't seem revelatory.

On weekends, Susan and I took road trips.

We soaked inside sulfur hot springs that turned my silver bracelets black. We made love at night and ate toast for breakfast under peeling Eucalyptus trees. I found a job tutoring high school students in English and History after school. In the mornings, I worked on a series of stories about a band of high school dropouts like the ones I had taught in Boston.

While some aspects of my life began to flourish, Dad and I lost ground. Though we barely spoke, I kept arguing with him inside my head while walking down the street or driving to work. The imagined conversations were part of the long continuous dialogue that I had had with him for years—about Greece or the coup or our family. In all of them, unlike in real life, I had the last word. But they weren't satisfying.

Eventually, I flew to Texas for a weekend visit. Maybe we could find a way to be closer. We met at a Mexican restaurant. I was in my mid-thirties, and Dad was sixty-seven. He was older, his hair white, but he seemed as strong as ever to me. After talking about the weather and his new house, I brought up the CIA and the Greek dictatorship. I had done little research on the subject, but that didn't stop me. Based on the little I'd gleaned from friends— Daphne and Efi and my trips to Greece—I was convinced he had been involved in shadowy, unethical things. Who cared about the chain of command or the fact that Greece was his first overseas field assignment? Rational thoughts like these didn't penetrate and neither did his denials when he made them. He said he knew nothing about the coup. He said there was no torture in Greece. He said, he said, he said. What hit me hardest was the heavy feeling I carried around with me—for Mom, Evelyn, and now Greece, all of us trampled beneath Dad's heavy boots. It was disappointing to leave the restaurant without answers. I convinced myself there was no more I could do. He wouldn't tell me the truth. I was happy with Susan now. That's what mattered.

Finding a spiritual center helped me manage my disappointment with Dad. Flags from different world religions hung from the ceiling of a former Christian church not far from our house. People welcomed Susan and me. There was no sin, no hell, and no patriarchy. No dark Christianity like the Catholic churches Mom took us to growing up. No priests who spoke sternly of temptation and the importance of following commandments.

Life in California felt good. Like a refuge. I called Evelyn to try and patch things up. I told her I wanted to put my house on the market. She had a trust fund from Grandfather too. I said she should buy a house of her own.

For a while, everything sat fine between us. She liked the idea of buying a house. We talked on the phone almost every week. But then months passed with no offers. The real estate agent said there were boxes in the basement that needed to be cleared. I called Evelyn and asked her to move them. She hung up on me. I called again. This time, she yelled and told me that I was being insensitive, that she was being displaced again—this time, ironically, by me. I felt ashamed. Still, her anger seemed connected to something deeper. I couldn't unravel it all. As gently as I could, I told her she should see a therapist.

When the house finally sold, Evelyn moved out and we stopped talking.

I told myself I belonged in California. But all my former places continued to haunt me. At night, I dreamt of New England snowstorms, and during the day, the dry hills of Northern California reminded me of Greece. I found a language tutor, thinking that maybe speaking Greek would soothe me. We met every week and reviewed grammar. Sometimes we talked politics. I told her that my father had been in the CIA and had been stationed in Athens during the junta. She told me stories about people arrested by the dictatorship. She said the U.S. had been complicit. It was familiar—the stories she shared and the guilt I sunk into as I listened. All the U.S. had cared about was keeping the communists out of Greece at all costs. They arrested ordinary people. Dad had helped carry it all out. I tried to push away thoughts of cramped cells, of people being beaten by men with hard faces.

Not long after my visit with Dad, he left a message saying he would be appearing in a documentary about the invasion of Grenada back in the early 1980s. The fact that he was going to be on television talking about one of his assignments stunned me. It was another instance of him reaching out, of him trying. But all I saw was Dad talking about Dad. I couldn't take in the fact that, in his way, he was trying to reach me too.

I resisted watching the program at first. I wanted to push it away the way I pushed him away. Grenada wasn't a necessary mission. It was one of convenience, an excuse for President Reagan to invade and capture a small number of Cuban tanks. But hours before it aired, I gave in. It was that impulse again, the desire to find a way to bridge the distance between us. But that's not what I told myself. A good daughter would watch, I said to myself. I was just being dutiful.

The program began, and I watched a newsreel of President Reagan speaking to the press about the unfolding crisis. "American lives are at stake," he said. He talked about the danger of Grenada falling into Cuban hands. Then Dad's face filled the screen. He sat before a pale backdrop in a blue dress shirt. Glare bounced off his wire-framed glasses. The title "Senior Intelligence Officer – Covert Operations" flashed below. I felt a quickening of pride.

A mission reenactment began. A female spy in a wig and big, nerdy glasses posed as an American official sent to resolve the situation diplomatically. She was shown being driven around by a guileless Grenadian as she scoped out the scene, noting the information she'd later relay to Dad. Then Dad returned to the screen. He talked about the importance of the invasion. His hands came up from his lap, and his fingers fanned out, as if poised to catch a beach ball. He was in his element now as he described the breakup of the Soviet Union. He was a self-assured professor. I fell into a trance as he talked about the Soviets leaving Afghanistan, the tearing down of the Berlin Wall, and the dissolution of the Warsaw Pact as proof. "In retrospect," he said, his voice full and resonant, "the Grenada invasion in 1983 was the beginning of the end of the Cold War."

I snapped out of it. How could he say that? *It wasn't the invasion of Grenada that brought down the Soviet Union. It was the collapse of its economy.* When the program ended, I called and told him it had been an interesting program, but what I was really thinking was *same old Dad.*

16. My Blue Liver

A few years after moving to Oakland to be with Susan, I found myself standing on a corner in Taos, New Mexico. I'd come to celebrate Susan's mother's sixtieth birthday, but I wasn't thinking about that. I was thinking about what Susan had just said to me: "You need to go back into therapy." She said I needed help with my feelings about family. We were supposed to be meeting her brothers for lunch soon, but instead I was crying.

"We love you," Susan told me. "My brothers love you. My parents too. But it's like you don't see that."

Susan's eyes were soft, and I saw the concern. She was trying to help. I knew her family loved me. I didn't know why pain from my own family was overshadowing their warmth. Why it seemed to stand in the way.

"Okay," I said. "I'll go."

I met a therapist, a woman named Ann. She was easily six feet tall, with shoulder-length, wavy, blonde-gray hair. Her office was located inside a small building above a Pet Food Express. For the first minutes of our initial session, I tried to explain. I talked and talked and then stopped. It seemed too big.

"Why don't we meditate," she suggested.

It was a relief to sit in silence, to let go of trying to fix myself. I felt the cushion press against my lower back. When I opened my eyes again, Ann was sitting peacefully across from me, her eyes gently focused on the carpet between us.

I took in her ECCO sandals and the small silver clock resting on the wicker table beside her chair. Thirty minutes to go. I told her there was a family pain buried deep inside me, something I couldn't get rid of. "Like an organ, a liver or something," I said.

"Does it have a color?" Ann asked.

"Blue," I said, "like the ocean."

She said that whenever I felt this family pain, I should try to visualize it. See it there inside me. "It's not all of you. It's just one organ. You can stay in touch with your dad and sister and Susan's family, and when it gets difficult, picture your blue liver. Witness it."

It seemed odd to visualize family sadness as an organ, a liver, to see it suspended below my ribs, floating there. But it was helpful too. Ann had said I could stay in touch with Dad, that when the pain returned, I should witness it. It was an invitation to not shut him out. Months before Thanksgiving, I had sent Dad an invitation to our house for the holiday. I wrote out the invitation carefully on eggshell cardstock. I told myself he may not come, but I wanted him to. If he didn't, I would try to witness my disappointment. I hadn't seen him in two years. I took my card to the mailbox and dropped it inside.

Dad left a voicemail a week later. He said he and Cindy were too busy getting settled into their new place outside Washington, D.C. He didn't say, "No, we can't make it, but we're free for Christmas." He had never invited us to visit them either. Instead of witnessing my blue liver, I slipped into anger. I was being a good daughter, but he was incapable of being a good parent. Superiority was just another place I hid my sadness.

You shouldn't have expected anything, I told myself. Ann was wrong.

A month later, Dad sent a Christmas card addressed only to me. My anger flared.

"I live with a woman. Why can't he ever honor who I am? He's such a homophobe!" I ranted at Susan.

I called and told him he had to acknowledge Susan. "She's my partner. I don't want any more cards that don't acknowledge her." I was practically spitting.

"The card was for both of you," he said.

"Then put Susan's name on it," I said.

That September, I turned on the television and watched the World Trade Center towers fall. My first thought was, *Dad will think this is his fault, an intelligence failure that his work didn't prevent.*

I called Dad, but it was Cindy who picked up.

"Your father cried in his chair watching the footage," she said. "Our apartment is right across from the Pentagon. We can still see smoke."

When Dad got on, he sounded hobbled. I wanted to comfort him, but this was way beyond the scope of our usual conversations. If we had had a closer relationship, maybe we could have shared our sorrow, opened up more to each other. Instead, I failed to think of the right words. After a few minutes, our call ended. I thought about Dad over the next few days. I pictured him in his recliner, tears streaming his face. I tried to imagine how it felt for him to have spent his career trying to prevent an attack on American soil only to see one happen. And right across the street.

SPY

17. Inside the Water's Embrace

At a creative writing workshop north of San Francisco, I stared at the arid hills outside my cabin window and wrote long pages about Greece—my love for it, my feelings about the coup, Dad, everything. I had wanted to express this for so long. It was a modest essay, rough and scratchy like the fig leaves that once grew in our yard. I thought, *Done. Now I can put it away.*

But it wasn't done.

I searched online for writing workshops in Greece and found one near Corfu that boasted: "Write in the morning, eat lunch by the sea, and read your work at night!" I sent an email to one of the workshop attendees and asked if it was worth going. Amalía, a Greek-American living in Athens, wrote back immediately: "Don't bother. The teacher was asleep half the time. We watched goats eat on the hillside all afternoon."

Amalía told me she was writing about family secrets. I told her I had some of those. Our emails flew back and forth—a grown-up pen pal. I told her I used to live in Greece as a kid but didn't say when or why, which worked for a while until she got curious and asked what years I had lived there. If I told her we arrived in the late '60s, during the coup and the beginning of the dictatorship, she'd suspect my family had something to do with it. Not many Americans just happened to live in Greece during the dictatorship. I liked Amalía and felt I could trust her—I wanted to—so I took a breath and told her the truth.

Weeks passed without my hearing back.

I felt like a pariah, an extension of Dad's dirty secret.

While I waited for a reply, I decided to read up a bit on the coup. I found an article that laid out the basics. The days before the military took over were fraught for Greece. A centrist party, led by George Papandreou, had won a narrow electoral victory, but the king (a foreigner who had been appointed by European powers after Greece had won its independence) thought Papandreou was too left-leaning. There was also the matter of Papandreou's son, Andreas. He was a firebrand who criticized the U.S. and wanted Greece to be less dependent on the west. George Papandreou considered appointing his son to a role in the ministry, but the king objected and dismissed Papandreou. Political instability followed. A few months before another election in which Papandreou was favored to win again, a group of Greek military colonels stepped in. The only way to save the country from communism, so the thinking went, was to take over. And so they did. Many believed the CIA had helped the colonels come to power. George Papandreou was soon captured. He died under house arrest a year later. His funeral became a demonstration against the coup. It was attended by thousands. I didn't want to know more. I had read enough.

***

Months later, Amalía emailed without mentioning our last exchange.

She had started a writer's retreat called Aegean Arts Circle on the island of Andros, her ancestral home. "Come write about your childhood—in Greece." Her words sang out to me.

I sat on the back deck with Susan, empty cereal bowls and coffee cups cluttering the faded redwood table between us, and tried to decide what to do. School was out for the summer, and my tutoring load was low. I could reschedule the few students I had for the week I returned. That is, if I went. I told Susan the teacher was Dorothy Allison, *the* Dorothy Allison, author of *Bastard Out of Carolina.*

"Which means you should go," Susan said.

"But what would I write about?"

"Keep going with the essay you started at the retreat."

I felt an impending kind of doom. As if attending the workshop would open a Pandora's box and I would never be the same. I didn't want everything to change. My life was good, or at least good enough. It made all kinds of sense *not* to go. There was the expense of a last-minute ticket to Greece and the fact that I didn't feel my writing was ready for a big-deal teacher. In the end, the force urging me to go was stronger. I took out my suitcase and filled it with summer clothes. It was as if someone else was packing.

***

The port was quiet when my ferry landed on Andros, a ship owners' island that stayed off the tourist map. I walked to the hotel, grabbed my key from the front desk, and wheeled my bag into the room. Jet lagged, I fell into the bed for a couple of hours. When it was time for supper, I found the dining area. Amalía was there. We greeted each other shyly. I met the other writers too, and we talked about our flights and said a few words about our writing. Dorothy smiled and welcomed us, but I felt like an imposter. All I had were stories about outsider teenagers and a rough essay about shame and longing.

After dinner, everyone left for their rooms except Amalía and me.

We sat on the terrace overlooking a nighttime sea, a half-empty wine bottle between us. Her curly black hair blew across her face. "I thought you were a spy or a plant or something. That's why I never said anything after that first email. It's crazy here. I didn't email you back because I just couldn't deal with it. When you said your father was in the CIA, I hesitated. I did not believe you were real. The CIA is a bad word here. Everyone knows it green-lighted the coup all those years ago. The colonels who took over were CIA puppets. The U.S. called the shots. I didn't know if I could trust you."

"That's okay," I said, pretending that it was. I wanted her to know I didn't resent her for pushing me away. I told myself she was exaggerating, acting paranoid. But I felt it too. The CIA lurked everywhere, pulling invisible strings. The CIA was a dirty word, like she had said. Dad was dirty too. And so was I. All the shame ran together inside me.

The next morning, I found a note under my door. "Since your first email to me, I have had such mixed feelings. I felt anxious, thinking you were a 'test.' Life can be dangerous in Greece, as I said last night. But I always wanted to email you again. I felt you were a genuine writer, and I wanted that connection with another writer."

Amalía's warmth touched me. I slipped her note in between the pages of my journal.

It was still early, so I took the path down to the sea. Smooth stones pushed into my arches as I shook off my flip-flops. I waded into the cold water, and when it reached my knees, I pushed into it, letting my paddling arms take me deeper.

***

Dorothy came to the workshop the next morning and scanned the room. She said we needed to write what terrified us. Her eyes narrowed with intent. "If you're afraid, then you're exactly where you're supposed to be. Never avoid fear. Use it."

She invited each of us to read from our work. We went around in a circle taking turns. When the person before me finished, my hands shook. I'd never said the word *CIA* out loud to a group before. I felt exposed, as if Dad was in the room and could hear everything I said. I rushed through my essay without looking up. I felt everyone's eyes on me—especially Dorothy's. When I was finished, she leaned back in her chair and said, "I love to read about people I hate."

I fought back tears. Who did she hate in my piece—me or Dad? Either way, that meant my writing had failed.

During a break, Amalía led me to the pool. She pointed to a man sitting alone at a table under the thatched roof. "That's Nick Papandreou," she whispered. "His father, Andreas, became prime minister after the junta fell. A leftist. The U.S. hated Andreas even though his wife was American."

I watched Nick sitting quietly by himself, his legs crossed, and the roof shading his eyes. He looked so unassuming. Not the son of a firebrand, or even Greek for that matter. He was so pale.

Amalía said the "colonels," as they came to be called, were all set to kill Andreas, but the Americans intervened. "You two have to meet each other. Go talk to him."

"I wouldn't know what to say," I said.

"Tell him what you're working on. Say you're at my workshop."

Amalía peeled away and left me standing halfway between the pool and Nick's table. I could walk back toward the hotel, and he probably wouldn't notice me, but Amalía was right. What were the chances I would ever meet him again?

I approached Nick and said, "I'm a friend of Amalía's."

Nick looked up. He appeared to be in his 40s, strands of gray threaded through his brown hair.

I didn't know how to warm up to the subject of the junta, so I just blurted it out. "I used to live in Athens as a kid. My dad was in the CIA. That's what I'm writing about here at Amalía's workshop."

Nick squinted. "What's his name—your dad?"

"Mike Absher," I said, bracing to hear that Nick somehow knew Dad. And not in a good way.

A beat passed before Nick said, "Doesn't ring a bell."

Then he launched into a story.

"I met a man recently, an American doctor." Nick looked toward the pool. "The night of the coup, my father was arrested and beaten by Greek soldiers. In the process of being arrested, he jumped from the roof and tore open the large vein in his leg. Blood flowed. The doctor was called in to examine my father. He told everyone that my father needed to be stitched up ASAP or he wouldn't survive. The people at the table—Greeks, and Americans from the embassy—asked the doctor, 'In how many hours will he die?' This astonished the doctor."

Nick looked up at me. I stared back.

"A decision had to be made. Should they help him? The doctor tried to keep out of it, but when it looked like they might let my father die, he said he had to speak up. He asked, 'How would it look if the prime minister's son was allowed to die?' They decided to let him live. It was that doctor," Nick said, "who saved my father's life."

I stood there stunned, not knowing what to say or why Nick had just told me this story. Mostly, I was wondering if Dad had been one of the Americans inside that room.

***

Later that night, I played it all back. In my version, I saw my father pacing the room, trying to decide what to do. He stared down at Andreas, Nick's injured father, the agitator. He was a leftist. He was ambitious. He wanted to become prime minister, and if that happened, he'd let the country go communist. Nothing would stop the Russians from taking over the rest of Europe and then the world. Should he and the others let Andreas live? My stomach dropped thinking that it was possible, that maybe Dad had been in that room years ago. Maybe he did things like that all the time. Maybe I had no idea who my father was.

***

Toward the end of the workshop, I sat down with Dorothy for our one-on-one conference. I asked for feedback about the essay I had read in class. I wanted to know if it was ready to send out to journals. I braced myself to hear more disapproval.

"I think it's a book," she said.

I stared at her. This wasn't the takedown I had expected.

"You'll figure it out," she said. Her mouth curled into a knowing smile.

***

On the last day of the workshop, Amalía knocked on my door. "You should read this." She handed me a book. "It can help with your research."

Research?

I read the title of the book—*Europe's Last Red Terrorists: The Revolutionary Organization 17 November*—and stared at the cover image of a car engulfed in flames. I had heard vaguely about the terrorist group and how it assassinated people after the junta fell, people it thought had collaborated with the dictatorship—wealthy businessmen and newspaper owners. And spies. They had killed spies. My palms felt sweaty.

"A lot of people looked the other way if N17 killed someone who made a million during the junta, or some CIA guy, or some sadistic military asshole who tortured people." She said no one likes to admit it, but it was true. "You can give it back before you leave."

When Amalía left, I tossed the book onto my bed, grabbed my sunglasses, and walked down the winding road away from the hotel. The sea shone over my right shoulder. Thistle plants, tall and spiny with crowns of deep lavender, shot up among the brown grasses on both sides of the road. I passed an elementary school closed for the summer. A plastic cup blew around the base of a basketball hoop, its net missing. In the distance, tiny yellow flowers followed an invisible underground spring down a ravine. When I came to a low stone wall, I sat down to rest on its uneven surface. A lizard skittered across the hot stones and into the shadows, taking my courage along with it.

***

Susan arrived the day the workshop ended. After a few days, we caught the ferry back to Athens, arriving just in time to celebrate Greece's upset victory in the 2004 European Cup. They had beaten steep odds to win and now the whole city was in the streets, proud to be Greek. Car horns sounded, flags fluttered from balconies, and everyone cheered. Susan and I got caught up in the mood too. We lifted our glasses and toasted Greece, the underdog of underdogs.

The day before our flight back to the United States, I remembered Amalía's book and told Susan I needed to find a bookstore. She waited at a café while I wandered Syntagma Square, looking for an English-language bookseller. I found one behind the square and stepped inside its air-conditioned walls. An employee slouched behind a desk, reading. I felt panicky. *Just do it.*

"I'm looking for books about the junta and N17," I said.

"In the corner. I will show you."

The woman rose and led me to a row of books by the window. I scanned the titles until I found the same firebombed car from the cover of Amalía's book. My T-shirt stuck to my sweaty back as I handed over my euros. N17's members had been arrested and imprisoned, but I felt as if they hadn't, as if they were still out there somewhere, as if I was their next target.

18. How Can I Investigate My Own Father?

Back in California, Susan sat reading comics at breakfast. I told her I couldn't do this.

"I can't research my father and the junta," I said. "What if I learn something horrible?"

Worry darkened her expression, then passed.

"You can do it, baby," she said.

Okay, I thought. *I'll pretend I believe you.*

I climbed the steps to my garage study, opened the book Amalía had told me about and started to read. The year was 1973. Our family had returned to the U.S. by then, by the time students at the Athens Polytechnic University had barricaded themselves inside the school's compound and begun broadcasting messages against the junta across the airwaves. The military had been in power for six years. A crowd gathered for days outside the university gates in support of the student resistance. But the army feared that support for the students would increase and so it sent in tanks. A standoff ensued between the military and the students until the go-ahead was given for tanks to move into the compound. It didn't matter that students still clung to the bars of the gate. Nothing could stop the heavy rotating wheels from crashing through the metal bars and crushing bodies. Twenty-four people were killed. The day was the 17th of November.

One year later, the dictatorship collapsed. The regime had

never been popular, but it was its overreach in trying to join Cyprus with Greece that truly signaled the end. The colonels sent in forces to overthrow the Cypriot government which resulted in an invasion by Turkey. I remembered Daphne and Efi's words. Their story. The sadness in their eyes. In the end, the island became divided with Greek Cypriots controlling the south and Turkey occupying parts of the north. This was the final blow. Ordinary Greeks had had enough. The dictators resigned in shame over their failed takeover of Cyprus. Conservative politician, Konstantinos Karamanlis, returned from Paris to stabilize Greece as prime minister until the socialist party PASOK came into power in 1981. By then, N17 had started its assassinations. They were revenge killings targeting people they believed had collaborated with the dictatorship. High on its list were members of the CIA.

I lifted my eyes from the page. The morning fog had lifted and the sky was blue, but everything inside me was sinking.

N17's first target wasn't just any CIA operative. It was the agency's station chief, a man named Richard Welch. On Christmas Eve, after Welch and his wife had returned from a party, he was gunned down in his own driveway in Old Psychiko, the same neighborhood where we had lived. He may have died just blocks from our house. If we had still been living in Greece at that time, maybe N17 would have come for Dad too. I closed the book. *I don't need this*, I told myself. Welch didn't deserve to be killed like that. I abandoned my research, rose from my desk, and made my way back toward the house.

***

The next week, I decided to try again. I drove toward UC Berkeley, parked, and headed to the Doe Library at the heart of campus. Once inside, I paid for a community membership, slipped the card into my wallet, and made my way to the Greek history section where I started scanning titles. Periods of history marched from antiquity onward, most relating to ancient and not modern Greece. I spotted a thin blue volume: *The Rise and Fall of the Greek Colonels.* Jackpot. I slid the book from the shelf and found a chair.

The author claimed there had been multiple rumors of coups in Greece during the late sixties. One believed that a group of Greek colonels was plotting, another that generals were poised to take over, and still a third that the CIA was planning an overthrow. The author said the rumors about the generals and the CIA were both false. *Okay,* I thought. *Maybe there is more to it.*

In another book—*Warriors and Politicians in Modern Greece*— the author described the close relationship between the Greek military and U.S. during the fifties and sixties. The close connection could be traced back to when President Truman gave an address to Congress in 1947. His speech—the Truman Doctrine—made it clear that communism was the new enemy. If it wasn't fought wherever it existed in the world, disaster and calamity awaited. Freedom was on the line. An attack against any United States ally was an attack against America itself. Money began pouring into Greece to fight the communist influence there. Athens quickly became one of the biggest American intelligence centers. Similarly, many Greek military officers had been trained by the U.S. Army. The U.S. was taking a keen interest in Greece. I googled the author of the book about the close military relationship between the U.S. and Greece and saw that he lived in Northern California, two towns away from me. I scribbled down his contact information and sent him an email about my project.

Two days later, he got back to me and proposed we meet. I panicked. Was I ready to meet a scholar of modern Greek politics and history when I had only just started to research? I took a breath and emailed back, saying I looked forward to a meeting.

"Let's have coffee next week," he said.

I arrived early at the Starbucks in San Leandro, thirty minutes down the highway from Oakland, and grabbed a table in the corner. Soon after, a well-dressed man in his early sixties strolled into the café. We introduced ourselves and ordered coffees before settling into our chairs.

"I'm trying to find out what my father did or knew about the coup," I said. I told him my story, the years we had lived in Athens, my mixed feelings about it all.

He listened and nodded. He was a professor and an author. This was his field. I felt like an interloper. When I finished, he said he couldn't give me a definitive answer about the link between the CIA and the Greek military.

"But there's someone you should talk to. You're going to Greece, aren't you?"

"Maybe," I heard myself say.

"Well, there's someone you should talk to when you go. He knows about the CIA during the junta years. Talk to him. He's a professor of Greek history and a friend. He knows people you should talk to as well, a journalist who has covered the coup for years."

I thanked him as I wrote down the name of the professor and the journalist, even though I was sure I wouldn't be talking to either of them.

***

I ordered CIA memoirs from independent bookstores, tomes that could give me a feel for what spying was like—meeting informants and the use of psychological gamesmanship. I opened my journal and sketched out some scenes. In one, I placed Dad in Greece in the late sixties, just days before the coup. In this imaginary scenario, Dad entered a corner café. As soon as he did, his blond hair and confident manner gave him away as American, maybe even as a CIA affiliate. The city was full of rumors that the CIA was planning a coup, meddling in the country's affairs. I imagined Dad picking a table by the windows. He sat down and looked out at the overcast sky. Perhaps the street looked more deserted than usual. When the waiter came over, Dad ordered a Greek coffee, *medio*, with sugar. He tried his best to blend in. I pictured a car pulling up to the corner and flashing its lights. Dad shoveled change onto the table, left the café, and climbed into the waiting car. A moment later, it sped away.

My scene rolled on. I imagined the car came to a stop in front of a bar. Dad had to duck as he entered the small space. They ordered something. The driver talked about a hardship, maybe a family member who was sick. The driver explained that there was little he could do. He said Greek hospitals took his money and did nothing. He said something like, "There is no health care in my country."

Dad nodded and sipped his drink. When the man was finished talking about his sister or his mother or cousin, I imagined Dad offering the man a slip of paper, the name and phone number of an American doctor who could help. Maybe Dad said something political and compelling to convince this man to become an informant, something like, "Greek hospitals would worsen under the communists. Have you seen the hospitals in Bulgaria? In Albania? It's barbaric. You're better off dead."

Weeks later, in my imaginary story, they met again. Dad asked how the man's relative was doing. Then I pictured Dad moving on to what he needed most: information. I saw Dad's still eyes, eyes that belied the passion behind them. He mentioned a communist-affiliated union and asked the man when the next meeting would be held. The man didn't know but said he could find out. He wanted to help. He was grateful.

I pictured Dad the next day, bending over his typewriter at the office. His informant had started to prove useful. Dad punched hard at the stiff black keys as he wrote his report.

"Communist Group Infiltrated" was its title.

***

The next morning, the red illuminated digits of the alarm clock read 6:00 a.m. I'd been awake for the last two hours. I pulled on jeans, left our bedroom, and made my way to the living room. I opened my laptop. When I typed in Dad's full name, an interview from ten years earlier came up. A graphic of a cartoon spy in a trench coat sat beside the title: "Cold Warriors Woo Generation X." I stared at the screen. My father had been floating in cyberspace since the mid-1990s, and I'd had no idea.

The interview took place in Dad's home in San Antonio, two and a half hours south of College Station where he currently lived. I pictured the gold-framed photograph of me and Evelyn from our days in Athens sitting on his desk. Dad started in about the class he was teaching at the University of San Antonio. "I've pulled no punches in this course. I've talked about intelligence failures, policy failures, everything. I've encouraged my students to make arguments against the continued existence of the CIA."

It was like I was reading the words of a total stranger. CIA policy failures? Encouraging debate about the continued existence of the CIA? This wasn't the dad I had known, the one who never failed to defend the rightness of the agency.

But there was one line that really got to me.

"Intelligence is my favorite subject."

It hit like a blow to the chest. I wanted Dad to say that I was his favorite subject. Or Evelyn was, or something personal, but he hadn't said anything like that.

The journalist in the article switched gears. He said there were plenty of missions Dad couldn't talk about. "...Absher can't very well argue for what he and his colleagues accomplished during his subsequent CIA postings overseas. Absher can't even say where he went."

That's more like it, I thought. *Dad and his secrets.*

But then, as if to try and disprove this, Dad brought up one of his postings—Vietnam.

The journalist said that in Vietnam, Dad had fought "a conventional war" against the North Vietnamese. "Absher zipped around his province in a helicopter and when necessary, called in B-52 strikes against suspected NVA [North Vietnamese Army] troop concentrations."

Dad ordered bombs dropped? I flashed to our conversation at the Mexican restaurant when I'd asked if he had ever killed anyone. He'd said then that he had "made decisions resulting in the loss of life." That sounded so vague, but now I knew what he meant. Vietnam. He was flying around Vietnam, ordering bombs to be dropped on troops from the air.

But what I read next stopped me cold. The article said Dad had supervised interrogations.

I stared at the page. Interrogations? Grim scenes ran through my mind—dank cells, prisoners who refused to talk, who got slapped around by men who lied and played mind games. Or worse. Much worse.

"I never saw any brutality," Dad added.

I leaned back in my chair, dumbfounded and staring out the dining room window until I heard Susan coming up from our bedroom downstairs.

After Susan made coffee and woke up a little, I revealed what I'd just learned. "My dad supervised interrogations in Vietnam. I just read it in an interview. He said he didn't see any brutality." Susan and I locked eyes.

Maybe Susan would say that what Dad had said was possible, that not all CIA interrogations involved torture. As a litigator, she came home each day having spent hours scrutinizing the real world. She pored over documents, looking for evidence, scanning depositions for inconsistencies, unraveling harrowing stories and facts and events. She knew about the ugly side of life, defending clients in product liability or medical malpractice cases. We had argued about some of her cases when we first got together. I asked question after question until I understood her ethics, could trust that she was who I thought she was—not the kind of lawyer who looked the other way, opting to win at all costs. I trusted her read of world events, her analytical mind, and her fairness.

"No brutality?" she asked. "That's hard to believe."

***

All day, I thought of faceless interrogators kicking and punching prisoners inside my mind. At night, my dreams were filled with them. In one, Susan and I walked down a sunny Oakland sidewalk holding hands. I leaned into her and whispered, "We have to be careful what we say these days." Just then, a man dressed in black stepped out from a tree and threw his hands over my head, a length of wire between his fists. He jerked the wire back, and in one clean motion, severed my head from my neck. There was no feeling as my head left my body.

Later, I told my therapist about my dream.

"Fear is something we need to honor," she said. "It moves alongside us."

I didn't feel fear moving alongside me. I felt it up ahead, leading me.

Back at the UC library, I picked up a book from the special orders desk. Without realizing it, I was starting to slip into obsession, into a state of mind that would take over my life. At the beginning, I told myself it was a manageable research project, a series of questions I already knew the answers to. But the day I opened a book called *Barbarism in Greece*, the library and all its college comforts and murmuring students fell away, replaced by the Greek colonels and their dirty practices. I learned the colonels had used hundreds of prisons during the dictatorship. Some were large municipal buildings in the middle of the city, like the infamous one I had read about on Bouboulinas Street, a busy thoroughfare in Athens. Others were located on small, barren islands. Priests, mothers, union members, communists, and leftists were all taken to these centers. In the first year alone, starting in 1967, just months after we had arrived, thousands were detained. Some were tied to benches and beaten; others were hung upside down as guards struck prisoners' feet with wooden sticks or metal pipes. Each scenario fed the next and the next, like one long and continuous nightmare.

As I read, I scoured for the names of the torturers and constantly felt like quitting. *Do I really want to know this?* I thought of contemporary "black sites," torture cells located in places like Egypt, Romania, and Afghanistan, convinced I would learn that U.S. spies had conducted the torture in Greece, but the book I was reading didn't suggest this. It said the Greek security police and Greek military police were the ones doing the torturing there. Not the CIA.

I checked out the book and headed home. Accounts of pain and despair followed me. I felt like they were tied around my waist, each one a link in a long metal chain. The torture wasn't abstract. It happened in Greece, my first home, the place I had felt I most belonged. Even if the CIA didn't do it, did they know and authorize it? Did Dad?

When I got home, the stack of dishes in the sink overwhelmed me. I attacked them with a vengeance, furiously slamming plates around, knocking over a bottle of cooking oil in my wildness.

Susan came into the kitchen. I didn't look up.

"What's wrong?" she asked.

"Torture," I said. I knelt down and started swiping at the oil with a wad of paper towels.

Susan made a move to comfort me, but I shook my head. I lifted the towels, heavy and dripping, stormed over to the trash, and heaved them inside. I didn't feel Susan's love. All I felt was fury.

19. No Show

It was spring 2005, six years since I had moved to Oakland and many months into my research. My pages were piling up, so I decided to enroll in an MFA program for support and focus. I sat inside workshop rooms with students fifteen years younger than me. I raced through my days, trying to keep my life balanced, giving Susan attention, still working with students, and getting to my homework. When Susan brought up planning our commitment ceremony, it seemed like a good idea. A way to take back some of my life from the Greek junta.

Susan agreed we could honor our coupledom in an expansive, non-patriarchal way. We brainstormed where to hold our event and who to include on the guest list. I went back and forth about inviting Dad, but decided that yes, I did want to include him.

I called to let him know about our plans. I was forty years old but I still felt like a child when it came to him. I could already predict his lack of enthusiasm. I asked how he was doing, and he started in on the house he and Cindy had just bought.

"It sure is a lemon," Dad said.

I pictured Dad's jaw set with irritation. They always seemed to have house issues. It kept them moving from one place to another, sometimes within the same city. They moved almost every year.

"So, what's new with you?" he said, switching gears.

"Susan and I are planning a commitment ceremony," I said.

"Oh?"

"We're planning it for the end of October. We'd love for you and Cindy to come."

"I'll make a note of it," Dad said dryly.

Anger flared in the center of my chest. I pushed on, saying I wanted to visit before the ceremony so that he and Susan could meet.

"I'm not sure that's such a good idea. We're trying to sell this house, and it won't be easy with all the problems it has. It's not a great time for a visit."

"We can stay at a hotel. How about early June?"

"It's not a good time," he said again.

Tough shit, I thought, but said instead, "I'm sure we can work something out."

I told Susan about the call later.

"I can't believe he said, 'I'll make a note of it,'" I said. "He has to deal with me. He doesn't get to just avoid us like that. We're going. Maybe you can meet Aunt Anne too."

***

Two months later, Susan and I flew to San Antonio. I had told Dad we were coming. To take the pressure off, I said we had planned other activities too. I didn't want him to think we needed them to entertain us the whole time. It was early summer and already broiling when we stepped off the plane. I called Dad's cell to say we had arrived and to see about setting up dinner plans, but he said dinner wouldn't work.

"How about breakfast tomorrow then?" I asked.

He couldn't make that work either.

"Lunch?"

"It's not a good time. I told you that. We have meetings about selling this house."

He was always busy—my whole life there had always been something. This wasn't about the house, anyway. It was about me. My sexuality.

"I'll call again tomorrow," I said and hung up.

When I called the next day, he relented. We arranged to meet at the USAA Towers, a residential community for U.S. military personnel where he and Cindy were renting an apartment while they repaired their house.

Halfway there, my phone rang.

"Sorry, but I'm not going to be able to make it today," Dad said, his voice cold.

"But we're almost there!"

"I told you not to come."

"What an asshole!" I screamed after hanging up.

Susan said we should just forget it, but I said, "No way." I was fuming, my hands locked onto the steering wheel.

We made our way back to our Victorian-style, gay-owned inn and collapsed onto the bed. I curled into Susan's arms and cried. It felt good to grieve. I felt a sense of relief too. The visit was over, and I could relax.

Since it was Pride that week, we changed clothes, checked the directions, and headed over to a downtown intersection. We arrived at a roped-off area where people either danced or gathered at fold-out tables, relaxing. It was a nice feeling—to be out in San Antonio—a place I usually felt closeted.

The next day, my determination took over. I called Dad again. He started right in with more excuses, but I cut him off.

"If you don't make time for this visit, it will really take a toll on our relationship." I didn't say, "I might not ever speak to you again," but that's what I meant.

"Okay," he said after a pause. "I'll meet you there."

Hours later, I felt queasy. He didn't really want to see me or meet Susan. He had only agreed because of my emotional arm-twisting.

Susan and I arrived early and stepped inside the marbled lobby of the USAA Towers. We found two leather chairs in the corner. A few minutes later, I saw Dad. His face was haggard as he planted his cane and shuffled over. There were dry spots on his forehead and more age spots on his hands than I remembered. We embraced, but the distance between us stayed in the center of our embrace, between our bodies.

Susan shook Dad's hand, but he seemed distracted.

"Cindy can't make it," he said. "She's in a meeting with the realtor."

He started moving toward the dining hall. Susan and I followed. We arrived at an empty room. The hostess came over and told us the kitchen was closed.

"Even for a sandwich?" Dad's words were clipped.

"Let me ask," the woman said, disappearing through swinging metal doors.

I panicked. What if they wouldn't serve us?

"Selling a house is such a pain," I said, trying to be supportive. Dad shook his head.

I shot Susan a quick look.

"I'm happy to seat you, sir," the hostess said when she returned. She took us to a table in the center of the deserted room. I sat across from Susan, and Dad sat facing the windows.

"So, how long have you and Cindy lived in the Towers?" Susan asked.

"Not long," Dad said without making eye contact.

Susan made a few more stabs at small talk, asking about the workout facilities, but Dad didn't bite. I felt small, the way I had as a girl. I wondered if it had been worth it. I had forced his hand, but at what cost? When the food arrived, it was a relief. By the end of the meal, Susan and I were carrying on a conversation with each other while Dad stared into space.

***

A week before the ceremony, after everything was arranged, I got a voicemail from Dad. "We're not going to be able to make it," he said.

I was too worn out by the emotional effort to care. It would be easier, anyway.

When Evelyn arrived, I was relieved. It had been months since we had last talked. I didn't know how to fix us but I was grateful she came. I wished Linda were there too, instead of stuck in Alaska teaching. Susan's parents, her brothers and their wives, her niece, three nephews, an uncle, and a cousin all arrived. They showered me with love, and I was grateful. The sun shone, and our guests circled around us on the deck. Susan's father stood near the reverend from our spiritual center. Evelyn approached the tall ivory candle and lit it in memory of Mom. A friend stepped forward and read a poem I had written about my love for Susan—*I want to wrap myself in a white cloth and make you a plate of cut cucumbers. I want to swim with you in an open pond and tremble when grasses brush our legs.* Another friend sang Paul McCartney's "Calico Skies" in a beautiful gospel voice, and our nine-year-old nephew played a song on the violin, his face focused and intent. Our niece held flowers. Susan's mother smiled, her eyes shining and her face open and happy. We cried, blessed our guests, and they blessed us. Afterward, everyone feasted on smoked salmon and homemade cupcakes. I was held up by all the love and good wishes and felt the Great Spirit surrounding us. The Great Spirit minus one.

A week later, Evelyn called me from her house outside Boston.

"I talked to Dad. He asked me how the ceremony went. I told him how great it was and beautiful. I wanted him to know what he missed, to get the picture that he should have been there." I heard the edge in my sister's voice, and I loved her for it. Sometimes, I felt that edge directed at me, but not this time. This time, she was on my side.

A month or so passed before Dad and I spoke. He asked how I was, and I said I was fine. We both glossed over the fact that he hadn't attended the ceremony, as if it was a simple thing to avoid, a familiar crack in the sidewalk.

***

On Sunday, Reverend Joan stepped to the front of the church and began her address. She said she used to think that if she could just get rid of the problematic people in her life, everything would be fine. Light glinted off her glasses as she looked around the congregation. "But cutting people out never really fixed things for me. The same problems just cycled back in the form of another person who pushed the same buttons. Eventually, I had to ask myself, 'What is this person trying to teach me?'"

All I could think of was Dad. She was talking about Dad.

I thought about my secret writing project. I had no idea where it was going, or *if* it was going, but maybe I could talk to Dad about it, mention it a little in our next call as a way of staying engaged.

I called Dad the following week.

When he picked up, he told me about their brand-new house and how much work they were doing—making the showers bigger, putting in grab bars. "It's a big job—I'll tell you that."

He sounded rushed, like he didn't have time to talk.

My pulse quickened. *Keep going*, I said to myself. "I've been doing some research about Greece during the junta, the years we were there."

"That's interesting," Dad said.

He didn't say more, and we hung up a few minutes later. I felt relieved. At least I tried, I told myself. I had brought it up—said I was researching the junta. What would I have done if he had dug in and asked me questions? Would I have told him more? From the little I shared, there was no way he could have known the whole truth—that every day I spent hours researching the junta and looking for proof of his guilt. Telling him about my project didn't change anything. In fact, it didn't seem to have any impact on him.

But then a couple of weeks later, Dad called me from the road. He said he was in Washington on special assignment.

"What's the assignment?" I asked.

"A breach of security. An American official killed overseas." He sounded energized. He said he had been called in by the Secretary of State to participate in the review process. "The job doesn't pay much, but it's the least I can do. If there's any way I can help prevent another death, then it's worth it."

The fact that he was picked by the Secretary of State was impressive. I wondered about the specifics and if the breach was in Iraq or Afghanistan, but I knew he probably couldn't say. Still, I was surprised he had told me as much as he had. The bulk of the mission stayed undisclosed, but he had shared some of it, the non-secret part, with me.

"Okay. Well, good luck," I said.

20. A Name

Researching the Greek dictatorship had become a full-blown compulsion. At first, I simply wanted answers to my questions about the coup and Dad's involvement. A part of me still wanted this—to expose his guilt. But another part, maybe the bigger part, wanted something more basic. To just know him. I wanted to feel the same way I had felt as a girl, the fleeting but satisfying experience I had the night he brought out the Viet Cong flag and told me what it meant. He opened up then, shared something important, something at the core of his being. The feeling I had in that moment hooked me forever. All I wanted from then on was to be let in. Trusted. But I didn't realize this yet. I hadn't yet made the connection between my desire to re-experience that moment and what was propelling me through endless hours of research. I was too caught up in the hurt of that first lie. Thirty years on, I still dreamt of "gotcha" moments, instances when I would have Dad cornered, when he wouldn't be able to squirm away. I could unmask him then and say, "I know what you are."

And yet, at the same time, I didn't want to know. I hoped there would be no "gotcha moment." I wanted my investigation to come to a close and to have found nothing or very little. I wanted my life intact, some semblance of a relationship with Dad.

A Greek-American historian who lived in Athens said I should file a FOIA (Freedom of Information Act) request which would give me access to federal records. He said if I wanted to see documents my father had filed, or files that pertained to his work at the CIA, this would be the way to go. I stared at his words on my computer screen. A FOIA. Of course, this was the way to proceed, to be a serious investigator. Was I a serious investigator and this a serious investigation? I felt conflicted each time I looked up the word "CIA" in a book or online. Or searched for my father's name. Sometimes I felt like a real investigator and other times merely a daughter looking for answers. Who was I anyway?

I talked to Susan about applying for a FOIA. She wanted to support me. She said I could do this, that maybe it would provide me with answers. I deserved to know and that a FOIA might help me a lot. But as she talked, I felt myself shutting down. It would mean making a formal request. What if my father was notified of my request? The idea that this might be the case overwhelmed me. Even if he wouldn't be officially told, what if he found out anyway? What would I say to him then? Somehow with the FOIA, I felt like I had to choose. I was either a daughter or a researcher.

"Okay," I said to Susan. "That makes sense. I'll think about it."

But after we talked, I felt myself shelving the idea. It wasn't a hard and fast decision. It was a gradual slipping away. I was still a bad daughter, but I hadn't crossed some invisible internal line. And this meant that I could still look things up online. I could still research books. *I'll consider a FOIA later*, I told myself. *First, let me see what I can learn on my own.*

***

One day, after following a particular trail of the junta for hours, I came across a name I recognized: Peter was one of Dad's best friends in Greece. I remembered Peter from growing up. We visited his house in Athens and then later in D.C. I had always liked him. I stared at the page. It wasn't the fact of Peter's name that shook me. It was what the book, *The Rape of Greece*, by journalist Peter Murtagh, insinuated that Peter might have done—given the Greek dictatorship the green light to overthrow Cyprus.

I went over everything relating to Cyprus and the fact that the Greek military had been in power for years at that point—seven long years of repression and imprisonment for anyone who dissented. And the U.S. had played right along. At first, the official U.S. stance was that the Greek colonels should return to their barracks and restore the country to democracy. But when that didn't happen, the U.S. accepted them as a necessary partner. At least the colonels were anti-communist, the thinking ran. So, when the colonels decided to try and unite Greece with Cyprus, a longtime dream of theirs, they turned to their partners in the U.S., specifically their contacts within the CIA. Would their coup be tolerated, or would they face some sort of punishment if they took over? According to the page I was staring at, they were contacted right before the attempted coup by none other than Dad's best friend, Peter.

The author wrote, "The key questions in this whole affair were whether the US administration, specifically Henry Kissinger, knew what was afoot, and whether the CIA was involved. The evidence is at best conflicting but sufficient to bolster claims that the answer to both questions may be yes."

I stared at the page.

The coup did happen. And if Peter was the one sent to stop it, he failed. But the relationship between the CIA and the colonels was so close, and had been for years, that if the CIA truly wanted to stop the coup couldn't they have? Had Peter been the one who delivered the message? And if he was, did he warn against the coup or say the U.S. would look the other way?

I stopped reading. The insinuation that the CIA contact—in my mind, Peter—may not have adequately tried to dissuade the colonels from attempting a coup was enough.

I left my writing desk for the house. In the basement, I found a box of old photographs. After sifting through a stack, I found one of Peter at his daughter's wedding in France. A long line of people stood outside an old stone building resembling a castle.

Peter stood at the end of the first row in a suit with arms that were too long. He smiled his lopsided smile, the one I remembered. He looked out of place at the fancy event, a Greek standing among French aristocrats.

Peter used to make me laugh. Whenever our family visited his, he teased me good-naturedly and called me by my nickname, Wessie. But now my memory of Peter was being replaced with a new one—someone who may have given the Greek military junta the green light to overthrow Cyprus, which then led to a calamitous invasion by Turkey. People died and were displaced. Neighbors became enemies—all because the Greek colonels wanted to fulfill their nationalist ideal. I thought again of my old friends Efi and Daphne. I remembered their pained stories about the barbed wire barrier that divided the island after the Turkish army invaded. A line that divides the island still.

Peter did this to them. I walked around the rest of the day feeling numb.

Like a clairvoyant, Dad sensed my crisis and called. "Haven't heard from you in a while."

"I found Peter's name in a book," I said, skipping our usual small talk.

"Peter?"

"The book says he may have been the go-between for the colonels and the CIA. He may have given the Greek military junta the green light to overthrow Cyprus."

"I don't know anything about that," Dad said.

"No?"

"No."

The air stilled between us.

"Okay. Well, maybe the book is wrong." But I didn't think it was. And I didn't think Dad thought I doubted its veracity either. We talked another minute or so, but the call was over. I had touched a nerve and I knew it.

The next week, I bought *Charlie Wilson's War*, a book about how a CIA spy and a congressman had teamed up to arm the mujahideen in Afghanistan in the '80s. The spy, a man named Gust Avrakotos, was the son of Greek immigrants from Aliquippa, Pennsylvania, a steel worker's town. Gust had previously been stationed in Athens during the junta. According to the author, *60 Minutes* producer George Crile, there were two CIA stations in Athens back then, an official one and an underground one. Gust, the book said, ran the underground one. Crile described Gust as bare-knuckled and crass. A working-class spy among men who, like my father, had gone to Ivy League colleges. Gust called the blue bloods he worked with "cake eaters," and he knew all the colonels personally.

I wondered if Dad had known Gust, and if so, which CIA did Dad belong to? The underground one or the one that followed the rules?

I called Dad, determined to bring up *Charlie Wilson's War*. I felt like I was on a roll, like I was getting somewhere in my gotcha campaign. "Ever heard of *Charlie Wilson's War*?" I asked a minute or so into our call.

"I'm not sure," Dad said, hedging.

"There's a section that talks about this guy named Gust Avrakotos. He was in the CIA during the years we were there. Maybe you knew him?"

"No, I don't think so," Dad said.

His non-committal answer rang false. Why didn't he simply say he had never met a 'Gust?' Why not just deny it?

Later, I thought more about the exchange. He had probably been vague on purpose, a well-worn evasion technique. More spy tricks. But it made me more obsessed about the connection between the Greek military and the CIA. I went onto a U.S. government site and found a bunch of PDFs related to congressional appropriations to Greece—money the U.S. gave to the Greek government and military. I skimmed through reams of dry documents until I came across something—an acronym. I leaned back in my chair and stared out the window. A tiny hummingbird floated above a branch. I looked back at the screen and read the acronym again.

That's when it clicked.

Twenty years ago, when I was getting ready to go to Athens for a semester, Dad came into my room and rattled off a string of words. I had no idea what he had been talking about then, but I did now. The string of words spelled out JUSMAGG—Joint US Military Aid Group, Greece. On the website for the U.S. Embassy and Consulate in Greece, I read, "JUSMAGG played an important part in channeling over 6 billion dollars in Marshall Plan post war and Cold War security assistance aid to Greece from 1947 to 1997." Where had I seen JUSMAGG before?

I walked over to my stack of junta-related books and flipped through the one about the terror group N17. I found a list of the people it had targeted. There it was. Two of its victims had been connected to JUSMAGG. The first official had been ambushed in heavy Athens traffic and was killed along with his driver in November of 1983. A second person was attacked in the same way less than five months later in April of 1984 but had managed to escape. This second attack, the unsuccessful assassination, occurred just months before my semester in Athens. No wonder it was on Dad's mind the night before my semester abroad.

I finally understood what had happened that night so long ago. I was about to travel to Greece at a time when U.S. officials, especially people connected to JUSMAGG, were being assassinated. Dad must have thought that if he told me this word, flagging it for me, that I would at least know it was a dangerous term, one that could potentially bring me harm. Maybe I would never come across it while I was studying in Athens, but if I did...

"Whatever you do, don't mention it to anybody," he had said to me as I shoved another wool sweater into my suitcase years before. It had been a warning. He had been trying to keep me safe. My father didn't just lie to me. He tried to protect me too.

21. CIA Interview

When I realized he had been trying to protect me all those years ago, I relaxed. Maybe I could say more about my research in our next call. Maybe I could trust him more, ask him about his career.

The next time we chatted, we made some small talk and then I said, "I have some questions about your work with the agency." My voice sounded tiny inside my head.

"What do you want to know?" Dad asked.

My palms sweat. I looked down at the list of questions scribbled into my notepad.

"What made you decide to join the CIA? I mean, why not some other agency?"

"Well, I was working in the San Antonio city manager's office, but my heart wasn't in it. The Cold War was really heating up, and I was scared. I thought the days of the United States were numbered. I bought a plane ticket and flew to D.C. I interviewed with everyone—AID, FBI, Department of Defense, the Peace Corps. It turns out none of 'em would have me because of that eye injury I got as a kid."

"You applied to the Peace Corps?" I had known about his eye injury and the fact that he once applied to the FBI and Department of Defense, but this was the first I'd heard of the Peace Corps.

"I did."

It stunned me to think that instead of a father who met with confidential informants, I might have had a father who helped build community centers and schools.

"So, what happened?" I asked.

"They wouldn't take me, and neither would the FBI. I'd already been in the Army in '58 but I couldn't advance because of my injury. The Army told me that if I wanted out, I could use my poor vision as an excuse. I told them why would I want to do that? I wanted to stay in the military. If I could have been an officer, I would have made the Army my career. Heck, I was proud to serve."

I scribbled all of this in my notebook as I listened. I wanted to hold onto the trove of information Dad was sharing.

"But like I said, they all rejected me because of my eye."

"How did that happen again?" I asked. I liked this story but I also needed time to catch up on taking notes and wanted to keep him talking.

Dad launched into it, explaining how he and Tom had been horsing around, jumping on each other's beds, when suddenly Dad lost his balance and went flying toward the window. He landed on it, and his eye hit the sill. My grandparents flew him to Houston for an operation. Afterward, he had to lie completely still for hours. Dad said it was December 7th, 1941.

"Boy, I sure remember that day. The Japanese had just attacked Pearl Harbor. After a couple of weeks, the doctors took off my bandages and said I was healed, but that the vision would always be poor in my right eye."

"You couldn't stay in the Army, but what made you decide to interview with the CIA?" I asked.

"Well, I knew they were on the front lines of the Cold War. And they were the last interview I had lined up. I've told you about that, right?"

"Tell me again. I love that one."

Dad launched into one of the few stories he ever shared about work. He said his interview took place inside an old Army barrack. "There was a guy who looked like a stern prep school dean sitting behind a desk and a brightly colored bird on a perch in the corner. I can't remember if it was a parrot or a toucan." The man started asking questions—Where had Dad gone to college? What was his major? And every time he asked a question, he grabbed a sunflower seed from the mound in his hand and tossed it at the bird. "That bird caught everything—fastballs, line drives, curveballs."

Dad and I laughed.

"When the guy was through, he said he couldn't tell me much. He couldn't tell me where I'd work or what I'd do or who I'd associate with. He said, 'After what I've just said, why the hell do you want to join the Agency?' I told him, 'I have no idea. You haven't told me a thing.'"

"He said, 'Good answer!' Two weeks later, they sent me a letter, and that was it."

"That was it?"

"Yep."

I'd heard this story over the years, but I felt like I was hearing it differently. Growing up, Dad had been so focused and decisive. Now I saw my twenty-something father, undecided, open. Joining the CIA hadn't been a calculated act at all. More like a giant leap of faith. He accepted a job with an agency he knew virtually nothing about. The decision that determined his life and shaped so much of mine was the result of happenstance—a random interview with a guy and a bird.

Back then, the CIA, along with other agencies including the FBI, were respected. They were seen as organizations where good American men and women worked to keep this country safe. The scandals of COINTELPRO, in which the FBI ran covert and often extralegal counterintelligence efforts to spy on American citizens deemed "subversive" from 1956 to 1971, hadn't come to light yet. Neither had the Iran-Contra Scandal in the 1980s, when the National Security Council (NSC) became involved in secretly selling weapons to Iran in order to fund a covert war in Nicaragua, transactions that were prohibited by Congress. The CIA was seen as upright then. Behind the scenes, it had already played a role in deposing a leader in Iran and manipulating the political process in the Philippines. But these events weren't on the forefront of anyone's mind then. America, and by extension the CIA, was seen as a positive force by many. That included my dad, a young guy who had exhausted many of his options. I pictured him sitting eagerly across the desk from an interviewer, a pile of sunflower seeds, and a parrot. His dogged desire to be a part of something bigger than himself made me realize that perhaps tenacity was a genetic trait.

22. Are You Recording This?

Dad and I started to talk weekly after the bird story. Each time, I asked another question and scribbled down answers as fast as I could. I moved back and forth between competing agendas. One moment I was trying to catch him in a lie, and in the next I was asking about his life and just listening.

"What was your first assignment with the CIA?" I asked.

"I started out with the Office of National Estimates during the Cuban Missile Crisis. It was my job to analyze the Soviet buildup. I read reports from all over the world and watched the whole crisis. Do you know what happened in '61?"

"The Bay of Pigs?" I asked, unsure.

"Yes, but also a Soviet cosmonaut had successfully circled the Earth, which meant the United States was losing the space race. That was a bad year. Kennedy and Khrushchev threatened war in East Germany, and the Berlin Wall went up. Plus, we learned the Soviets were testing missiles *in the atmosphere.*" Dad's voice pitched up, and I heard the same Cold War panic I had heard as a girl.

One afternoon, toward the end of one of our calls, his tone changed. "Say, are you recording me?"

"Just taking notes," I said.

"Because if you were, I'd have to go over a few things for accuracy."

I stopped scribbling. What did he mean he would have to go over things "for accuracy?" How could a recorded answer be amended for accuracy's sake? Wouldn't that make it a different answer altogether? I felt like a fool. I had started to listen to him. I was so hungry to know more about his life that I didn't notice him slip away. He wasn't "Dad" anymore. He was the spy dissembling. And I was a kid being lied to again.

I found Susan in the kitchen after Dad and I hung up. She was chopping on the cutting board, preparing a stir fry.

"My dad just asked if I was recording our conversation. He said that if I were, he would have to go over things 'for accuracy.' I can't believe he said that." I felt a sob rising in my throat.

Susan opened the cabinet over the stove and pulled out a bottle of vinegar.

"He's fishing around, trying to figure out if he needs to be worried about what he's said." She splashed vinegar into the pan. "If you recorded him, he would probably want a copy of that record so he could control how he gets portrayed and what happens to his words or any allegations that might get made. It makes sense."

She grabbed a wooden spoon and stirred the sauce, then looked up at me.

"It feels shitty," I said.

***

The next week, my Greek-American historian friend emailed me a batch of interviews from an oral history project—people who had worked at the U.S. embassy during the junta. Dad and I had been talking. Things felt a bit better between us. The thought that at any time I could learn something I didn't want to know dogged me. *Do I really want to keep going?* I wondered.

But I did. I opened the file and printed the pages. Hundreds of sheets landed inside my printer tray. I sat down to read. Most of the people interviewed seemed anodyne and offered little insight. I kept reading until I came across someone different, more outspoken—a political officer named Robert V. Keeley, an

American diplomat who went on to become the U.S. ambassador to Greece in the mid-'80s. He said that while he didn't think the CIA had orchestrated the coup, he did say the colonels—Greece's soon-to-be-dictators—had been meeting and plotting *for years*.

Dad had always said that the United States had no idea the colonels were plotting a coup. But that was a lie. As usual. Keeley went on to say that there were lower-level, Greek-American intelligence officers, including some in the CIA, who were sympathetic to the colonels. He said that one of these officers might have known what the colonels were up to and decided intentionally not to report it. I thought about Dad's best friend, Peter. Or Gust, the rogue CIA guy.

Susan was watching *Grey's Anatomy* when I came into the living room. It was almost 9 p.m. I'd been working for hours, not even stopping for dinner.

"I found info about some Greek-American CIA officers who might have known about the coup and let it happen," I said, without even giving her a kiss hello.

She stared.

"What's wrong?" I asked.

"I feel like this has taken over everything. It's all you think or talk about. It's like you don't even think about me anymore. Or us."

She was right. I felt the junta swirling inside my brain all the time. I tried pushing it away sometimes, but it was always there, humming inside me.

Don't fuck up the best thing in your life, I told myself. *Take a break from the junta.*

But when Susan left for work the next morning, I kept going. Keeley, the diplomat, had said there were U.S. government reports that revealed the fact that the colonels had been plotting for years. I needed to find these. But did I really? I felt as if they would lead me to a culminating moment of truth, one I wasn't sure I wanted to face. And what would really be revealed anyway? We would still be a father and daughter who didn't visit each other, who saw the world so differently. It was too late to change the fact that he had spent hours away from home when I was a kid—tied up at work and unable to come to my soccer games or meet my friends. It was all linked together inside me, but I didn't see this. Catching him in a lie had become my way of trying to make him see me, even when I felt conflicted about it. My weird way of bringing us closer.

I went to the State Department's website and clicked "Greek/ U.S. relations" from a drop-down menu. Hundreds of files came up. At first, all I found were endless diplomatic cables. No secret meetings. Nothing about a coup.

I changed the search dates to the late '60s and something popped up—a State Department report written just months before the takeover. The account described a meeting of a group of Greek military personnel, stating that the group had been meeting since 1963—*four years* before the 1967 coup. The report's anonymous author said that this particular meeting had occurred just months before the coup, and what's more, Papadopoulos, Greece's soon-to-be dictator was present. According to the report transcribed from the meeting that night, Papadopoulos talked about the stalemate in parliament. He said that if the political situation continued to deteriorate "...drastic action, i.e., dictatorship, will be needed."

I stopped reading. The proof I had been looking for was right there. I had spent almost two years trying to confirm my suspicion that the U.S. knew about the impending coup and had done nothing to stop it. Now, I had my answer. The report was authored by the State Department and not the CIA, but it all blended together in my mind. If the State Department had known, surely the CIA did too, I reasoned. Government agencies became one inside my mind—the State Department, the CIA, the U.S. embassy. I'd met with scholars and spent hundreds of hours at the UC library, reading and highlighting documents, looking for proof that the CIA/U.S. had known about the coup, that they were the bad guys or at least players in that action, and I was right.

Anger stormed inside me. Dad. The one who lied to me and didn't make time for me and who didn't come to my commitment ceremony. Peter. Gust. The official CIA. The unofficial CIA. The U.S. government. The State Department. They blended into one culprit. They all knew. The United States was guilty of complicity with the dictators. They must have also known about the people the junta tortured too—men and women who wanted their government back and who were severely punished for speaking out.

You have to call him, I told myself. *You owe it to yourself. And to Greece.*

"I found declassified documents," I said after Dad picked up. "The State Department has a field report showing that the colonels had met covertly for years before the coup. You said we didn't know about the colonels, but we did. It's right there on the government website."

My voice wavered.

I was twelve again, standing in hip-hugger jeans, a long ponytail hanging down my back, telling Dad that I had finally figured out his steel ring trick. He had batted me away then, but he wouldn't be able to do that this time.

Dad's voice stayed even. "That's not what I said. What I said was that we didn't have any *specific* information about a *specific* group of colonels. We had a lot of suspicion in those days. There were always military plots." I felt like Dad was gone. The government spokesman was back, giving me the official line—gaslighting me again.

"I found something else," I said, moving on. "There's somebody who worked in Athens during the coup who says Greek-American CIA officers might have known about the coup ahead of time but decided not to tell anyone about it. He says it's possible they let the coup happen because they were sympathetic to the colonels."

Peter and Gust's names sat unspoken between us.

"This guy can say what he wants. He's entitled to his opinion. You have to be pretty careful, honey, if you're trying to build a case around something like that."

Dad said "honey," but his voice was hot with suspicion. If we had been in the same room, he would have pointed his index finger at me.

"You're asking a lot of questions about the colonels. Why are you so interested in them?"

"Because it's part of my life," I said. "Because we were there."

23. I'm Sorry

Confronting Dad about the CIA's involvement in the Greek coup had been a culminating moment for me. It took weeks to recover from feeling lied to again, from the energy it had taken to call him. But it wasn't the same for him. He was used to debate and deflection. When he called a few weeks later, we talked about the usual pleasantries. I didn't tell him I had bought a ticket to Athens for June. Or that once there, I planned to meet Greek scholars and visit junta-related sites. I wasn't even sure I wanted to go through with it now. After all my research and preparation to confront Dad about the coup, he had stuck to his denials. No gotcha moment.

The next week, I was in my car after a student appointment. It was raining hard. I watched water rivulets stream down my windshield as I dialed Dad's number. It was the middle of the week, not a time I usually had a lot of success reaching him. I didn't think he would pick up, but he did.

"Can you tell me a story?" I asked. "Maybe something from Greece. Nothing big."

"Let's see . . . I remember getting into an accident one day in front of the Hilton. Did I ever tell you about that?"

I said I didn't think so.

"Well, I was near the city center when a police car jumped the median and careened into a line of cars, including mine. We weren't injured, me and the Greek guy I was traveling with, because we were wearing seat belts—but my car was totaled. I ended up buying a '67 Ford Mustang with the insurance money. A beautiful car. Boy, I should never have sold that one. That car would be worth a fortune today!"

I tried to imagine Dad driving a muscle car and not the safe family cars of my childhood. Still, this wasn't what I wanted. I wanted a family story—the time Evelyn ate part of a houseplant and Dad brought the whole huge plant to the hospital so the doctors could know exactly what she had eaten. But when I asked about that day, he said he didn't remember it. My next student appointment was starting soon, so I told him I had to go.

A few hours later, I decided to call again. Maybe there was more to the Hilton story. I called back and said I hadn't been taking notes in our earlier call. "Can you tell me that story again?" I asked.

Dad went through it again. When he got to the part about how much money the Mustang would be worth today, he stopped. "Say, can I ask something?" he asked.

"Okay," I said.

"What made you so mad at me years ago?"

I froze. He was talking about us. Our relationship. I didn't know exactly what he meant though. Was he thinking about something specific?

"You mean growing up?" I asked

"Right. What was that about?"

My heart hammered. The question was so sudden and its scope so vast.

"It was kind of an accumulation of things," I managed to stutter.

"Right. Can you tell me more about that?"

I had no idea what to say. My list of lifelong disappointments— grievances I'd told therapists and friends and Susan, but never Dad—stretched wide inside me. The commitment ceremony felt too recent. And raw. So did all of his lying about his job and Greece. I needed something simple, a thing concrete enough that I could point to.

Just then, the call dropped.

"Dad? Hello? You there?" I tilted the phone back and forth. I pushed the redial button, and it went straight to voicemail. *"Malaka!"* I screamed, cursing in Greek. I hit the redial again, and this time it went through.

"Sorry," I said. "The service isn't great today. It's raining."

My mind raced through all my disappointments again, big and small—feeling lost and alone when Mom died, being dragged around from place to place, him being completely unsupportive about my sexuality. Everything sat unaddressed inside me. I felt like I couldn't breathe. Dad was waiting. I had to say something.

"There was that time you were driving through Boston on your way to your high school reunion. You and I had plans to meet at a café. Do you remember that?"

"Okay," he said.

Great. He didn't remember that, either. "I was on my way to meet you. My friends were already there. I wanted them to meet you too, but before I got to the place, I pulled over at a pay phone to check my messages. There was one from you saying you weren't coming. That was hard. You didn't show up."

My eyes stung with tears, as if it had happened just yesterday.

"I'm sorry," he said, then paused. "I should have made the time."

It was a single small apology. Over the next several days, I replayed it inside my head. I marveled that Dad had been the one to bring up our relationship, not me. It was a table-turning that I still couldn't quite grasp. How could the words, "I should have made the time," matter so much? But they did. Decades-old anger faded in an instant. He wasn't the enemy in the same way anymore. He was just Dad. I thought about canceling my trip to Greece. Maybe I could let go of my research now. I wanted to be done with it all. But the Greece of my childhood still needed answers. I wouldn't be going back for him. I'd be going for me.

24. Athens Pride

It was the summer of 2006 when I arrived in Athens. Jet lag from my ten-hour flight combined with the dry air to sap my energy. I dragged my bag from the carousel and grabbed a taxi in the waiting line. Minutes later, we glided away from the airport. Susan and I had made up from our fight. She didn't like the fact that I would be gone a month before she would join me at Amalía's workshop, but gave me her blessing anyway. The workshop, the whole reason I started this writing project, had been two years ago, but it felt more distant. As the taxi zoomed toward the city center, we passed a billboard that announced: Welcome to Greece! Create Your Own Myth!

I read over the directions Andrea had sent me; I'd be staying with her for the next four weeks. The taxi entered the winding streets of upscale Filothei, where pink and white oleander bushes lined the roads. The driver and I spoke in Greek as we searched for house numbers, passing proud homes hidden behind tall gates and thick tree cover. I spotted a place protected by a high metal fence and thick hedges that matched the description in the email.

"*Na to*," I said. That's it.

I paid the driver and made my way to the front door. A tall woman with shoulder-length strawberry blonde hair opened it a moment after I rang the bell. As we talked and introduced ourselves, Andrea pushed down a black-and-white spotted dog that insisted on jumping onto me.

"That's Max," she said.

I bent to give him a scratch and found a bare patch of skin on his side, pink and hairless.

"Someone threw acid on him. I found him at the airport and brought him home. I couldn't just leave him there."

Andrea invited me inside.

The house was dark, sealed away from the heat of the day by heavy curtains.

"Thanks so much for letting me stay with you," I said.

"It's not a problem. I have a huge house. Much bigger than what I need. I told the embassy I didn't need so much space, but this was what was available."

We sat on the sofa and talked about how we both knew Amalía.

"All expats know each other here," Andrea said. I wondered what Andrea did at the Canadian embassy, but I didn't ask. Instead, I told her I had met Amalía online and had attended one of her writing workshops on Andros.

"Oh, there's something for you," Andrea said, bolting off the sofa. She went to the dining room table, picked it up and returned.

"Amalía left a phone for you to use while you're here."

"Thanks," I said. I told Andrea more about my research into the connection between the CIA and the junta, something I had mentioned in my email. "I'm trying to reconcile what my dad did or didn't know back then."

"Bombs are still common here," she said, looking away. "It seems like there's one every week. Two of my colleagues were targeted. Their car was set on fire then pushed off a cliff while they were in a restaurant, eating. We're all careful here."

Fear pricked the back of my neck. I wasn't in the U.S. where Greece's Cold War coup hardly registered. I was *here* where it still mattered a lot.

Andrea went into the kitchen and came back with a bus schedule. She told me where the nearest stores were and which buses went to the subway. Then we went downstairs, to the separate apartment where I'd be staying. It was dark and cool. I set my bag down on the bed.

Before I got up the next morning, Andrea had gone to the embassy.

I put on stretch pants and a T-shirt and did an hour of yoga. I stayed inverted in a headstand as long as I could, breathing deeply. It felt good to do the poses, to have a way to steady myself. Afterward, I carried coffee, feta, and honey out to a yard that spanned three sides of Andrea's house. A short magnolia tree with open blooms grew on one side, pink oleander bushes on the other, and in the middle of the property sat a patch of grass. I spotted some planters. Most of the plants in them looked dead. One was so dehydrated I couldn't identify it. Probably just weeds. I dragged a hose over and filled it with water. When a small thorn caught my finger, I realized it wasn't a weed but a dehydrated rosebush. Roses used to fill the garden of our house in Old Psychiko. I wondered if they still grew there, if the house itself was still standing.

After breakfast, I scanned my list of the places I planned to visit—the embassy, the Hilton Hotel, our house, and one of the detention centers used for torture. I read the two words I had circled and underlined: *Find Anna*. Now that I was here and had a place to stay, the reason I had come overwhelmed me. My Greek was intermediate. And the only people I knew here were Amalía and a friend from the Bay Area I would be meeting at Pride in a few weeks. Other than that, I was on my own. I checked my watch and saw it was too late to call Susan. I glanced at the list again. Maybe I could handle the Hilton.

I put my journal and camera into my messenger bag and left for the bus stop. It was early but already hot, so I kept to the shade. At a kiosk, I bought a ticket. Minutes later, the bus rolled out of Filothei toward the city center. I imagined Dad standing beside me as the bus turned onto Kifisias, the wide avenue that led downtown. It was the same route Dad had taken to the embassy forty years ago, the same street where N17 had gunned down its targets, pulling up to them at streetlights and putting a bullet in their heads. If Dad was here beside me, I wondered if the avenue would conjure fond memories of living and working in Athens, or if it would bring up frightening images of American officials killed on their way to work.

I switched to the Metro, and two stops later arrived at the hotel. The Hilton had been a hotbed of CIA and American activity back in the late '60s. I felt a stab of fear as I crossed the wide avenue and pushed open the glass door at the entrance.

Once inside, I bypassed the front desk and made my way toward the far end, where I could look around without being watched. At the back of the open, airy space sat a white leather sofa shaped like a large tear. Piped-in piano music pinged against the marble walls and floors. A floor-to-ceiling bank of windows looked out at an infinity pool, luxuriously empty. I longed to be in it, swimming laps, my arms moving in a steady rhythm. Above the pool, flags waved—the blue and white flag of Greece, the Hilton Hotel flag, and another that read Oasis. This was where Mom and Dad had brought out-of-town guests.

Before my trip, Dad and I had talked about the Hilton. He said back then you could order an American-style burger or a BLT sandwich there. "Maybe you still can," he said. Now, looking out at the patio beside the pool, I tried to imagine him inside the vault of time, ordering a cheeseburger and waiting for an informant. This Hilton was new. It bustled with a contemporary European energy. I couldn't locate its old American vibe. Not anymore.

***

A few days after I arrived, I rang Dad. He greeted me by saying, "*Yia sou korrrri mou*," letting his *r* roll extra-long. Hello, my daughter. His playfulness irritated me. I was sick of him being sweet, goofy Dad while I was the bad daughter who investigated her own father.

After telling him I had arrived safely, I asked if he knew the address of our old house. He said he didn't. All he remembered was the street name. I decided my next stop would be the embassy. I could find our house some other day.

I took a train to the Megaro Mousikis stop on the Metro and started walking up a smog-choked boulevard. A few blocks later, I spotted a formidable structure encircled by a tall metal fence. I stopped a passerby and asked in Greek if that was the U.S. embassy. He said it was. I thought of the demonstrations that happen here every year commemorating the fall of the junta, Molotov cocktails thrown against stone and metal to protest U.S. complicity. Terror seized me. Surely everyone would know my secret. *You're fine*, I tried to tell myself. *No one can tell anything.* But just then, a pack of uniformed guards rounded the corner to my left. They marched straight at me in heavy boots. My stomach dropped as I braced for a confrontation, but they passed me without making eye contact.

In the near distance, beyond the current shiny embassy building, I made out a small guardhouse and a glass door that led to another modest-looking building, one with tall, unprotected windows. It was the old embassy. The door at its front must have been the entrance Dad used in the sixties, before all the demonstrations forced the embassy to move into a bigger and better-protected building. I pictured Dad swinging through the door in his black wingtips, navy blue slacks, and suit jacket. America was a shining idea then. Not what it had become for so many in the years that followed—the country that orchestrated the coup.

***

The streets in front of Parliament were blocked off for Greece's second-ever Pride. It was Sunday, and the whole square felt deserted; I'd never seen it so empty. I had plans to meet up with Tina, my Greek-American friend from the Bay Area. We'd only known each other a short time, but she felt like a sister. Tina turned to a few friends she'd brought with her and introduced me. We headed over to the march, where there were no crowds or onlookers. Still, it was a big deal, like it used to be in the United States in the early nineties. Except no one was in drag here, and there were no floats. It was Greece's second Gay Pride done the Greek way—politically left and without frills.

A few hundred or so of us marched with bullhorns and banners blazing. It felt exhilarating to be so out in Greece. When the march ended, we arrived at a small square lined with tables and booths stacked with political pamphlets. An older woman approached us.

"What's happening?" she asked in Greek.

"We're marching for gay rights," Tina's friend told her.

"What? What are you doing?" the woman asked.

Tina's friend was dubious. "I just told you."

The woman stood waiting.

The friend rolled her eyes. "We're lesbians. I'm a lesbian."

The woman suddenly backed away from us. Her shopping bags swung wildly from her wrists.

After looking at books and signing mailing lists, we found a restaurant with tables set up in an alley and ordered beers. We laughed about the woman, but it was sad too. Maria, one of the Pride March organizers, sat beside her girlfriend and spoke in English, telling a story about growing up gay in Greece.

"I'm one of the lucky ones," she said. "My mother was never like that. I became a super dyke because my mother was so accepting. She was that way even when I was in high school."

Maria turned to her girlfriend and asked if she needed anything. When her girlfriend raised her eyebrows, the Greek signal for no, Maria returned to her story.

"This one night, I had plans to go out with friends. My mother had no problem with this, but usually, you know, I put away all my little toys and books. And believe me," she took a puff on her cigarette and tilted her neck to blow smoke up away from the table, "I had a lot of toys. My mother, she was accepting, but I didn't want her to know everything."

The girlfriend took the cigarette from Maria's fingers.

"Maria!" a voice called from a nearby table.

"Mano! You didn't call me, you idiot! Where were you?"

The two of them went back and forth in rapid-fire Greek. A second later, Mano was gone, and Maria grabbed the cigarette back from her girlfriend.

"But anyway. That night, I didn't 'straighten up,' as they say. When I came home the next morning, the door to my room was open. I knew my mother had gone into my room, but she was acting so normal. Everything was okay. So I asked, 'Did you go into my room?' She said, 'You mean, did I find all of your disgusting toys?' For a second, I thought, who is this mother? She is a monster! But then my mother started laughing and said, 'Your toys are so big!' We laughed so hard, we almost peed our pants. That is the kind of mother I have."

We ordered another round of beers and smoked and told more stories, and for the space of an afternoon, I felt the freest I had ever felt in Greece.

25. The Spy Himself

I got up early and ate toast in the gray light of Andrea's kitchen, trying not to get anything on my blue dress shirt. After weeks of phone tag, the San Leandro scholar's contact—the professor of Greek history—had agreed to meet with me. I took the bus to the Metro, and thirty minutes later, arrived at his office. The day was hot, and I fanned my face, hoping I didn't look too dragged out by the heat. When I informed the receptionist I had an appointment, she led me into a small conference room. A minute later, a middle-aged man with salt-and-pepper hair dressed in khakis and a polo shirt breezed into the room.

"Nice to meet you. Please sit," he said in perfect, relaxed English.

I chose a chair near the head of the table.

The assistant came in and gave us each a glass of water.

"Thanks so much for meeting me," I said, taking out my notebook. "As I mentioned, I'm writing a memoir. I'm researching the connections between the CIA and the junta. My dad was in the CIA and was stationed here. I'm trying to understand what he knew. I guess you could say I'm trying to reconcile it all." The idea of writing a memoir felt real then as I said the words out loud; my search for answers seemed worthy.

The professor nodded and said, "Those were pivotal years for Greece. By this, I am referring to the Cold War. Imagine what would have happened to Greece if it had fallen behind the Iron

Curtain after World War II? We would be like the rest of Eastern Europe. Your father was an important man."

I felt suddenly thrust into an argument.

"Okay," I said, "but I read a theory that some in the CIA knew the colonels were plotting a coup and decided not to tell their superiors or try to stop it."

"Have you read *Charlie Wilson's War?*" he asked.

"Parts of it," I said, suddenly wishing I had read it all.

"Well, as you know, it's about Afghanistan, but there's also a section in it about the Greek junta. After the coup, the colonels arrested many politicians. Among them was Andreas Papandreou, the prime minister's son. He was on the left, of course, and considered a threat, but he was also educated in the United States. He had connections, and so there was pressure for the colonels to release him. The CIA sent one of their own, a Greek guy named Gust Avrakotos. They told him to deliver a message saying that they had better release Andreas. He was simply too high-profile to be detained."

The professor paused and peered at me.

"And you know, of course, what this guy Avrakotos did. According to the author of *Charlie Wilson's War*, Avrakotos told the colonels he had an official message and an unofficial message. The official message was to release him. 'But,' he said, and here's where he delivered his unofficial message, 'my advice is to shoot the bastard.'"

A bemused smile spread across the professor's face.

"They released him, but this story illustrates the fact that we can never really know what happens in the field. There will always be officials who do things of their own volition, without an order from their superior. Sometimes, despite orders from their superiors."

Avrakotos should have stuck to his job, I thought. He shouldn't have delivered his own personal message. The problem in the world was that there were all these little dictators running around. Some wore army uniforms. Some didn't.

The professor took a sip from his water glass and smiled. "I can tell your reading has been very compartmentalized. You don't know your stuff. Your research is incomplete."

"I'm sure someone could find weakness, but I'm doing the research."

"Ah, that's right. You're a writer, not a scholar. I was being a little provoking. I'm sure your book will sell like hotcakes in the U.S."

Sell like hotcakes? I had told him on the phone that I was writing a memoir about my life, not some kind of spy thriller.

"There's a journalist named Papahelas that I'd like to talk to," I said. "Can you help me contact him?"

"He's very busy. To talk to him, you would have to bring him information. Perhaps something your father has told you."

The professor leaned toward me in his chair, waiting. It took a beat for me to realize that he, too, wanted information, something Dad had shared with me, the inside scoop on the coup. It was never me he wanted to speak with, the daughter reconstructing her life. It was Dad, the spy himself.

"I don't have any secrets," I said and watched the light in the professor's eyes dim, his interest in our visit over. *And even if I did,* I thought, *I wouldn't tell you.*

26. Not Your Usual Museum

The next day, I was still too unsettled by my conversation with the professor to do anything junta-related. I picked up a pamphlet of museum listings and skimmed the exhibits. Nothing interested me. I was about to chuck the pamphlet onto my pile of newspapers when I caught the name of a place I'd never heard of or even imagined existed: the Museum of Anti-Dictatorial and Democratic Resistance. My pulse quickened.

"We close in an hour," a man said when I called.

I rushed to the bus stop and climbed on just in time. The schedule said we left in three minutes, but I watched as the driver opened his paper and spread it wide across the steering wheel. The three minutes ticked by, and all he did was turn pages. *Drive the fucking bus*, I wanted to scream. There was no emergency to arrive that afternoon, but I was caught up in it, propelled by a need I couldn't fully identify. It was as if my relationship with Dad waited for me at the museum. The future of it or the resolution of it; I couldn't tell which.

The driver kept reading so I closed my eyes and distracted myself by picturing the museum, something state-of-the-art—items displayed inside glass cases and a shop to buy postcards. It was stupid to think I'd find the answers there, imprinted on some placard that said, "The CIA did not know about or plan the coup and here is proof," but I hoped for it anyway. Or maybe there would be a list of the CIA officers suspected of setting up the coup and Dad's name would or wouldn't be on it and it would all be over and I could stop this obsessive investigation.

I heard the bus engine spark up, and I opened my eyes.

Fifteen minutes later, I arrived at my stop. I jumped out and hiked to the top of the park to a medium-sized municipal building. Inside it, a man sat behind a low desk, clearly bored.

"Is this the Anti-Dictatorial Museum?" I asked, out of breath.

"Did you call?"

"Yes. Did I talk to you?"

He ignored my question and said, "One building back."

I dashed outside and found another municipal building. A plaque by the door read: The Museum of Anti-Dictatorial and Democratic Resistance. I had arrived.

Dust hung in midair inside the filtered sunlight of the building's narrow hallway. There was no air conditioning, no glossy gift shop, no modern café for well-heeled travelers. To my right, a line of grim photographs hung unevenly across a wall with peeling paint. From them, a woman with close-cropped hair and a man with downcast eyes, both with heavily bruised faces, stared somberly at the photographer—and at me. I heard voices from a nearby doorway. When I approached the threshold, the conversations dropped away. A group of older men sat in white plastic chairs along the wall, staring at me.

I asked if the museum was still open.

"You're the one who called?" a man with pure white hair asked, using slowed-down Greek as if speaking to a child.

"Yes."

"Do you know what kind of museum this is?" he asked.

My purple sun hat and camera gave the wrong impression. I glanced at the sparsely furnished room and at the serious faces. Besides these elderly men, I was the only one here. The plaque outside made it clear that I was in the right place, but there was something else implied by his question. The man's face was weathered, his eyes intense and sad. That's when I got it. I wasn't inside a museum in the usual sense of the word. I was inside a building that was once used for torture.

"I know exactly where I am," I answered, looking him in the eyes.

Another man, thin and energetic, jumped to his feet. "Come, I will show you our museum." He ushered me down a hallway that had no doors, only doorways and arches. A wooden partition stood inside the building's large central room. Someone had stapled old newspaper clippings onto it, ragged and brown.

The guard asked where I was from.

"*Ameriki*," I answered, kicking myself for not using the more politically correct but longer United States of America.

His face brightened, and he said something about Bill Clinton. I squinted. Maybe I wasn't getting his Greek. Why was he talking about Clinton?

He said Clinton had come to Athens when he was still president, and that people had protested the visit. He said something about the CIA too, but I couldn't catch it all.

"What did Clinton say?" I asked.

My guide's Greek sped up even faster, and I lost the gist.

"Did he talk about the junta?" I asked, trying to regain what he'd said.

"This is what I am telling you." A childlike smile crept across his face. "He apologized."

I knew Clinton had traveled to Athens, but I didn't realize that he had apologized.

Much later, when I sat down and played the footage of Clinton's speech in Athens, it felt like less of an apology and more of a basic acknowledgment of how the United States had allowed its interests in fighting the Cold War to overrule its "obligations" to uphold democracy. But that day, my guide's eyes shone. I saw what could happen when a U.S. leader, a former president, acknowledged a decades-old transgression of complicity in a brutal dictatorship. It was such a simple gesture but so redemptive.

Next, we entered a small room, no more than eight square feet. In the rooms we'd passed, I had noticed memorabilia. This one was empty. No furniture or photographs, just a bare cement floor. I felt a chill. A chain with a rusted metal sign hung across the threshold. I read the sign and breathed hard. *Kratitiria Basanistirion.* Torture Chamber. I couldn't focus on what the man was saying to me. I stared at the crumbling walls, the sagging chain. People were brought here, to this exact spot, and beaten on the soles of their feet for wanting their government back. I had studied the dictatorship and its torture methods, read books and articles, written about it over and over in my journal, but standing here made it real.

He pointed to a thin whip nailed to the wall and drew back his arm, released it, and drew it back again. I knew how whips worked. I wanted him to stop. He kept going with his cartoonish gesture, swinging his arm up and out.

"*Katalaves?*" he asked.

I said, "*Katalava. Katalava.*" I understand.

He pointed down the hallway, toward the room of old men. "We are all volunteers here for an organization."

I gave him my pen and notebook. "*Grapsto parakalo,*" I said. Write it please.

Hand shaking, he wrote out each word slowly. The script sat jagged like my heart: Union of Imprisoned and Exiled Resisters, 1967–1974.

They were all detained here. Or somewhere like here. The years I had lived happily and obliviously in Old Psychiko, the military police had detained and abused these men. And now they spent their days showing people flimsy display boards with brown newspapers that would soon turn to dust. I didn't know what to say to him or how to acknowledge what he'd told me, the pain inside the place where I was standing.

"Thank you for the tour," I said after he led me back to the entrance. The men in the room were talking to one another now. I turned toward the door.

"*To vivlio!*" My guide's plea made me turn back around.

He pointed to a small book on a stand. A long list of signatures ran up and down the pages, visitors from around the world. I stared at the last name, someone from Norway. Then it registered. He wanted me to sign.

Fear claimed me. What if one of the men recognized my last name? I wanted to push through my shame, push past all the questions I might never be able to answer and meet this moment. I wanted it to be my apology for things I didn't do but knew occurred. My own family implicated.

Dad's spirit hovered beside me. He leaned on his cane, waiting to go. I couldn't read his eyes, couldn't tell what he knew or would say if he were here. But he wasn't here. I was. I picked up the pen and wrote *Amerikanida sungrafeas*. American writer. Then my name. When I had first visited Dad while he lived at a CIA base, I signed my name to keep his secret. Today, I signed to break it.

27. Finding Home

When the bus arrived at the entrance to Old Psychiko, I got off, a printout clutched in my hand. I wanted to revisit my family's old house—and maybe discover some remnants of home that I hoped existed there. A week before, I'd returned to where I thought the house stood; before a dinner with Amalía, I had peered into the darkening yard, hoping something familiar might register. Though it could've been our house, nothing in my memory clicked satisfyingly into place. Afterward, I had asked Susan to email me a photo I left back in California, one with Mom holding me in front of our sturdy wooden door.

The door I was now staring at.

I pressed the buzzer to the front gate. A moment later, it swung open. A young woman who seemed like an employee of the household stood before me looking confused. I started reciting the phrases I'd practiced for weeks—how I used to live here as a child with my family and how I'd come back to research Greece—but before I could finish, she instructed me to wait and disappeared into the house. I stepped into the yard and sat down on a low stone wall. The last time I was here, inside this yard, I was five.

A moment later, a young boy came to the doorway and peered at me. I asked if his mother was home, but he ran back into the house without speaking. Then a teenager arrived. He stared too, until a woman in her thirties with short, light-brown hair, wearing jeans and a white linen shirt stepped out from behind him and greeted me.

"*Kalispera sas,*" she said. Good afternoon.

"*Kalispera sas,*" I answered. It was the middle of the day, *mesimeri*. A wave of self-consciousness came over me. It was lunchtime, and I'd come along and interrupted them.

"I used to live in your house when I was a child," I said, trying to smile as sweat ran down the center of my back.

"Which years?" she asked, shifting from one foot to the other.

"From 1966 until 1971," I said.

"I have photographs," I blurted out, remembering my proof. I pulled out the scanned photo Susan had sent, the black-and-white photo of Mom holding me in front of the door. I pointed to it. "See," I said. "It's the same as your door."

The woman took the paper and squinted at the image.

"This is my father," I said, showing her a second photo of Dad crouching down next to me on the sidewalk. "It's beautiful here. How long have you lived here? Can I take a photograph of your house?" I asked.

She shook her head, but said, "I can show you the garden if you like."

She turned and walked toward the front of the house. I followed behind. The pebbled yard was gone, and now there was a lawn.

"I remember a pond here," I said. "And a big backyard."

"The backyard plot was sold years ago."

I flashed to the fairy stories Mom had told me and Evelyn in the backyard. We came to the front of the house, and the woman stopped. I didn't know what was going to happen next. Was she about to say, "Well, that's it—the tour is over?"

"My mother died when I was sixteen. She wasn't able to come back and see the house," I blurted out. I didn't know why I had just said this. It felt like something too private to share with a stranger, but I felt emotional standing in my childhood home.

The woman watched me. How could I explain to her what coming back here meant? All I had were simple words, a functional but unsophisticated Greek. We stood in the yard without speaking. The white pebbles were gone. The fishpond was gone. Mom was gone. I looked up at the house and saw the steps leading to the porch. The house looked smaller to me now. In my mind, it had been majestic, but now I saw that this was a child's memory, a child's point of view.

"Come inside," she said. "I can show you the house."

My breath intensified as I climbed the stairs and stepped onto the polished parquet floors I used to run across as a kid. I glanced at the corner of the living room where our Christmas tree once stood, filled now by a sofa. Just ahead, in the dining room, a table was set for lunch. The two boys sat watching me from their chairs, their backs rod straight.

"There hasn't been much work done on the house," the woman explained, walking me past the table to the wood staircase that led upstairs. I followed her up the stairs to the landing, and we walked past each of the three bedrooms. I stole quick glances into each room as we passed. I wanted to take everything in but all I saw were beds and clothes and lamps and windows. They could be rooms inside any house, any home.

We descended the stairs back to the main floor, and I realized it was time to leave. Her sons wanted to eat, and she wanted to join them. I was about to thank her and say goodbye when I noticed a small sitting room on the other side of the dining area.

"Someone lived with us," I stammered.

"A girl?" she asked.

I wanted to say not a girl but a young woman who taught me Greek, who made me feel like I belonged here. I strained to think of a better word, like *nanny* or *caretaker*, something that would better convey what Anna meant to me, but I couldn't, so I just nodded.

"Is there a room downstairs?" I asked.

The woman was confused. "Why do you want to see this room? It's just for laundry."

Just like I couldn't explain to her why I was standing here in her house, I couldn't explain why I had to go downstairs. She had been kind, this woman. She had let me into her garden and house, but now there was one last thing I had to do. I spotted a set of narrow steps off the dining room and moved toward them. *Don't look back. Just go,* I told myself.

Within moments, I was following these stairs into a small cave of a room. Shirts sat folded on top of the dryer, and oversized detergent boxes stood in the corner. There was another set of steps that descended even further into the earth. All I heard was the blood pounding inside my ears. I was trespassing now, but I couldn't stop. I took this little staircase until I found myself standing inside a tiny afterthought of a room—a storage room—but I didn't see any of that. Instead, I saw my four-year-old self rushing into this space, into Anna's old room, carrying the book I had been studying for weeks.

"*Thiavazo! Thiavazo!*" I said back then. I'm reading!

Anna had put down the laundry basket and sat on her cot. "Show me," she said. She pulled me onto her lap, and it was as if nothing else existed but the two of us. I sounded out the words slowly, carefully. She smiled as I read, and when I was done, I felt proud and almost as Greek as Anna.

Back upstairs in this stranger's house, the teen and his brother were eating and talking now, but the woman was standing by the table, waiting.

"Thank you," I said, rushing past without speaking. I couldn't explain to her why I was crying. This was their home, but it had been mine too. The front door was still open. I moved toward it. A second later, I was down the steps and at the gate. I swung it open and stepped out onto the sidewalk. Cars circled the small rotary. A man shouted at someone from across the street. When the bus arrived, I climbed on and watched the tiled roof of our house recede as we made our way out of Old Psychiko, the past colliding with the present inside me.

28. Cover Story

I called Susan that day and told her about my visit to the house. Our daily calls were getting more difficult, each of us worn down by the distance. My need to follow this journey had pulled me away from her. Again. A month away was too long. "I'm sorry," I said. I felt my throat closing, choking off words. I had made plans and bought my ticket as if she wouldn't object. And she didn't. Not really. But it was the way I had just marched on, letting it take over everything. *Two more weeks*, I told myself. *Then she'll be here, and we'll never have to do this again.*

Later that day, I stood on a downtown street corner in front of a cold drinks case and pulled out a carton of peach juice. The kiosk's interior was dark and silent; no transistor blared with loud Greek pop. I slid my coins toward the woman seated inside and said I was looking for a café by the name of Zonar's.

"Gone," she said. She told me there were other cafés close by.

I said I was only interested in that one. "Can you tell me where it used to be?"

She directed me to a corner I had passed many times the last few weeks. How had I missed it? I thanked her and walked several blocks before arriving at a shuttered building. I took a step back. Could this be the café's old façade? A metal grate covered its tall windows, giving it the look of a slumbering face with shut eyes. I imagined it open and busy, the way it had been during my college semester, with waiters zipping around in white aprons delivering dark coffees.

I left the corner and climbed Lykavittos Hill to a hipster café with outdoor seating. After ordering a Nescafé frappe, my phone rang. When I picked up, Dad greeted me.

"I found Zonar's!" I said, excited. "Didn't you used to go there?"

"Almost every day. A great place. I worked right upstairs, where JUSMAGG had its offices."

It took me a minute. This was the body that funneled U.S. military and economic assistance to Greece after World War II and throughout the Cold War. It was the organization where two former officials had worked, officials who had been gunned down in traffic, assassinated by the terror group N17. Dad was saying he worked within JUSMAGG's office?

"So that was your cover?" I asked.

"Right."

I wanted to ask more, but I didn't. I let the disclosure sit where it was, simply stated and out in the open. I could almost hear happiness in Dad's voice. Was it because I was here? A country that he had once lived and worked in? A place I suspected he had loved and loved still? I told him I had gone back to our old house.

"That was pretty emotional," I said.

"I bet it was," Dad said.

We hung up, and I walked back over to Zonar's. I looked up at the windows over the café, to the offices Dad had come to every day to type out reports. I peered through the tiny holes in the grate covering the windows of the coffee house, but it was too dark to see inside. I sensed Dad there anyway, sitting at a table, his mind buzzing with thoughts he couldn't say. I saw my college-aged self there too, at a different table, mapping out a weekend trek to the countryside. Two different times. Two different journeys.

***

The next week, I arrived on Andros again. This time I had more than the small essay I had brought two years before about my father, the CIA, and Greece. I had a two-year writing project I hoped to move forward.

At the hotel desk, I picked up my key and scurried off to my room. Strong *meltemi* winds raced across the island. I lay down on the bed and listened to the wind scream beneath my door. Somewhere beyond my room, I heard another door start to close. First the creak, then silence, and then a deafening slam. It echoed inside me, that sharp slam. I dreaded tomorrow. More than anything, I dreaded seeing Nick Papandreou, the teacher. He was teaching the Aegean Arts Circle writing workshop this summer. I had read and been moved by his novel, *Father Dancing*. Still, I had no idea what to say to him. Would he remember meeting me by the pool two years ago? I wanted to learn from him, learn what it was like to be an introverted writer growing up in the shadows of politics, what it had been like to write a book about having a politically charged father. But his father—a socialist who became prime minister—was hated by the U.S., and my father represented that hate. I played out meeting him. *Hi, again, remember me? I'm the one with the dad who worked for the CIA, the organization that hated your father. How's it going?*

The next morning, I procrastinated by staying at breakfast as long as possible before going to the workshop room. When I finally arrived, Nick was there at the head of the long table. He introduced himself in English to the group of American, British, and Greek writers. He was soft-spoken and reflective, the way I remembered him. He said nothing about his famous family, just who he was as a writer. When it was my turn, my neck flushed. I said my father was in the CIA and that I was working on a memoir about living here during the junta. I felt everyone's eyes on me, especially Nick's.

"It's been almost forty years since then," he said, his eyes soft. "It's good to see the kids are finally talking to each other."

I relaxed a bit after that. Everything was fine, I told myself. But then, at the mid-morning break, Nick and I avoided making eye contact, and later, at dinner, he arrived with his wife and two small children and took the seat next to mine. Despite being so close, we talked only to our other neighbors, never to each other.

Back in my room after dinner, I felt stupid. What was I thinking, signing up for a workshop by someone whose father had been targeted as a CIA enemy? A man the CIA officer named Gust had supposedly advised to shoot, according to what the professor I had interviewed in Athens had relayed to me from *Charlie Wilson's War*. It didn't matter that I was writing about my complicated relationship with my father, just as Nick had written about his. I tried to stop my thoughts. Susan would arrive tomorrow. That was all that mattered.

***

The next morning, I walked to the port in time to see the wide metal ferry ramp lowered. People rushed to disembark. Finally, Susan appeared—in jeans and sneakers, round-bodied and beautiful. I wrapped my arms around her and gave her a kiss, even though people stared. We walked back to my room and dropped onto the bed. Tears slid down my cheeks.

"I missed you so much," I whispered.

At dinner, I introduced her to the other writers and to Nick. He smiled openly while shaking her hand. We were done with writing and so we settled into a dinner of grilled lamb and field greens and talked about other things. Eventually, the sky darkened into dusk. Beyond the balcony, near the horizon, a small sailboat slid across the sea, its sail outlined by a twinkling string of lights. The group fell silent as we watched it slowly disappear beyond the rocks.

After the workshop ended, Susan and I wheeled our bags down the crooked street toward the ferry boats. We climbed onto the ferry, took the stairs to the upper deck, and waved at Amalía, who took out a white handkerchief and waved back. People chain-smoked inside the crowded cabin, but we didn't care. All we felt was our good fortune to be on vacation. Arid islands drifted past as the sea swept wide and calm.

We disembarked on Tinos, where a throng of hotel employees with placards rushed the ferry. Susan and I tried to make our way through the glut, but I grew impatient. A man pushed his hotel placard toward me. "No, thanks," I said and kept walking. I wasn't about to get suckered into some tourist spot. I knew Greece; it wasn't my first trip here. Susan yelled at me from behind. I turned to see her five yards back.

"Why are you walking so far ahead?" she said, irritated.

I explained about hating the crowds at the port, especially all the sales pitches, but I had hurt her feelings. Eventually, we found a hotel, collapsing onto one of the room's full-size beds. I apologized for being a jerk and leaving her behind.

The next morning, we realized our room was too small. The only way to get from the door to the balcony was by raising our bags over our heads. We left in search of better accommodations and, after talking to some people in a café, located a family home with a room to rent. The only problem with family homes was the questions the proprietors usually asked. The first one would be why Susan and I weren't traveling with our husbands. Still, family homes were also where you could experience true hospitality, and I wanted Susan to know the real Greece.

I knocked on the front door, and a friendly thirty-something woman answered.

Alexandra introduced herself and invited us inside. A few minutes later, she brought out a dish of homemade almond cookies and started to prepare coffee. The cookies were delicious, but I knew what would come next.

"What brings you to our island?" she asked.

I told her we were writers and had come here to work. I said we lived near San Francisco in California, an obvious tipoff that we were gay. She seemed to take it in stride.

"Your cookies are delicious," I said, taking another.

I started to relax. Alexandra hadn't asked about our husbands or if we had any children. When we finished, she took us upstairs and showed us our room, tidy and clean, with two balconies. She opened the doors, and the wind rushed through the flat. After a few more minutes of polite talk, she said to let her know if we needed anything and left.

Susan and I started to unpack when a few minutes later, there was a knock on the door. *Here it comes*, I thought. When I opened the door, I found Alexandra holding a bowl of fresh purple figs. She said they were from her garden.

"*Kalos irthate*," she said. Welcome.

***

A week later, we left the islands for Northern Greece where one of my Greek tutors from the Bay Area owned a vacation apartment. Susan and I boarded an old train, a fifties relic, perhaps borrowed or purchased from Yugoslavia or the former Soviet Union—sparse and utilitarian. We placed our bags in the metal bin overhead and for the next five hours stared through scratched windows as the train heaved itself past thick green fields and dry expanses of dirt. In one village, boys kicked a soccer ball in the street. In another, a man on a donkey made his way down a dirt road that ran alongside the train. It seemed like nothing had changed in hundreds of years. The only evidence of modernity was the occasional shiny new car.

We pulled into Thessaloniki, and I peered through the dim windowpane, spotting my friend and her little girl waving from the platform. The four of us piled into her car and sped along the highway toward their small apartment at the seaside resort of Halkidiki. For the next few days, I forgot about my obsession with the junta. We went swimming every day in a sea that was calm and inviting.

Susan floated effortlessly and grinned. "Extra padding, very buoyant."

We both laughed.

After unwinding for a week, we took the train back to Athens. If I was going to find Anna, my nanny in Greece, I had to start making calls. My friend said it was possible. She said everyone in Greece was listed in a computerized telephone database, and up until recently, women were listed under their maiden names.

Susan and I left our downtown hotel and walked to an internet kiosk where I entered Anna's maiden name into the online telephone directory. Over fifty entries with her first and last name came up in Athens and nearby towns. I wrote down the numbers, inserted my prepaid phone card into a public phone on the street, and dialed the first number. Susan stood beside me, holding my backpack as cars roared by. The first Anna I reached was too young, and the next one said she had never worked for an American family. Each time I reached one of the Annas on my list, my breath shortened. But after an hour of calls, there was no Anna from my childhood. The impossibility of my search registered. To find her I would have to review government documents, birth records, death records—deal with the labyrinth of Greek bureaucracy. It would take years, and even then—because I wasn't Greek—I'd likely get nowhere.

***

Only a few days remained in our trip, and I'd gone to most of the places on my list—but not Bouboulinas Street, Athens' most infamous torture center. The museum I had visited weeks before had been used as a torture center during the junta, but Bouboulinas Street had been the main Athens detention center then. And if I was going to try to get in, I had to go now.

Susan offered to come with me, but I told her I needed to do this alone.

I kissed her goodbye and headed out of the hotel toward the Metro. During the ride, I reviewed phrases in my head—*I'm here to research the junta. My father worked for the embassy. I'm an American writer.* I got off the train, walked down the long avenue, and turned onto the side street behind the archaeological museum.

I entered a small goods shop where I had arranged to meet someone who could escort me into the old detention center, now a Ministry of Culture building.

But the proprietor said the escort couldn't make it.

I panicked.

"It's open. Just go in," he said to me in Greek.

The heat of the day pressed into me as I walked up the narrow street toward the red shutters. Three blocks later, I arrived at the front and saw people passing the guardhouse briskly. I kept my focus straight ahead and walked with purpose, as if I too had an appointment. The guard didn't look up from his cell phone.

Inside the lobby, people crisscrossed the drab tile entranceway. A young, friendly-looking, female security guard stood next to a metal detector. I hoped she was actually friendly. *Here goes,* I thought.

"I'm looking for information about this building during the junta years," I said in Greek. It seemed like my words didn't register, or maybe she had heard many people say this. She pointed to a door on the other side of the lobby and told me to ask someone there.

The room she directed me to was some kind of mail or filing room. People shuffled in and formed a line behind a stern-looking man in brown leather dress shoes. He forcefully stamped the papers people offered him. There was nowhere to sit and wait, so I loitered by the door while the stamping continued. Then the room emptied, and a lull took over. It was just me and the frowning bureaucrat. He pivoted toward me and reached out his hand to receive my document. I told him I was a writer and that I was looking for information about the history of the building during the junta. I didn't know how to explain my journey—the place that Greece occupied in my life, that I had come to honor the lives of those once imprisoned here.

He lowered his hand and stared at the floor tiles.

"Is there a plaque or a pamphlet I can read?" I asked.

He said nothing. Sweat dripped down my chest. Why wasn't there any air in this place? If I walked out now, he and I could both pretend I hadn't brought up the junta on a perfectly good and ordinary day.

"*Pame*," he said. Let's go.

I fell in behind him, and we quickly crossed the lobby, bypassing the metal detector and the guard. We headed toward the elevator. He pressed the button, standing erect and silent. The elevator took an eternity to arrive.

"Do you have Greek roots?" he asked in Greek. He kept his gaze on the elevator door.

I told him I didn't but that I had lived here as a kid. I told him my father had worked for the U.S. government.

"At the embassy?" he asked, offering the acceptable euphemism.

"Yes."

The elevator finally arrived, and we stepped inside. Two floors later, the doors opened, and the bureaucrat strode out. I moved quickly to keep up, following him down a hallway. File cabinets lined the dark, low-ceilinged corridor. At the end of the hallway, there was an open doorway, and we stepped inside. Two young women sat behind desks. The sides of the room were lined with metal chairs. I wondered if maybe this had been an interrogation room before it became an office.

The man dropped into one of the chairs and motioned for me to do the same. I tried to catch my breath. *I shouldn't have had so much coffee this morning.* I wanted to tell this man he could leave, that I could wait by myself. I was just about to say something to him when he got up, mumbled something, and exited.

The woman looked over at me and asked, "What is your request exactly?"

I told her what I had said to the man. She left the room for a few minutes then returned. The phone rang, and she answered it. I stared at the hazy windowpanes. Everything felt like an absurdist play. What was the purpose here? A second later, the door burst open, and a man in his early sixties, wearing a plaid blazer, walked in and greeted me. I stood up. He asked me what I needed, and I launched into my spiel. He didn't seem surprised. Maybe it wasn't an uncommon request. Maybe there were legions of journalists who came here from around the world.

"There's no one to take you on a tour," he said. "Perhaps another day. I am sorry."

I needed to see something, maybe just the roof, where I had read so many had been tortured back then. I wanted to whisper a prayer there for all who had been harmed. But he said going to the roof was impossible. I couldn't tell if he was angry or bored.

"That's all in the past. The building has been transformed. There is nothing to see."

He said more, but I didn't catch it all. We shook hands. The visit was over. I took the elevator back to the lobby and crossed toward the exit. The building closed in around me, expelling me out onto the sidewalk. I peered up at the roof. Its yellow and white striped awning waved at me. I thought seeing the terrace would give me a sense of resolution. But that hadn't happened. Instead, the whole thing felt like a failure. As if I was still holding onto a piece of history others had let go of. It was an office building now. Everyone had moved on but me.

29. A Punch in the Gut

Dad called shortly after Susan and I returned to California. He asked how it went, and I said it was fine. To make the point that it had been a working trip, and not just a vacation junket, I told him I had visited some detention centers.

"Did you visit any happy places?" he asked.

He sounded concerned, like he didn't understand why I would go to a detention center. He didn't get what I was trying to do, what I needed to do for years and had finally done. Or tried to do. My heart twisted for all the things that still sat unsaid between us. We had started talking a bit at least. He had apologized. Things were different between us now. All he wanted was for me to have had a good time, a father's wish. I told him we went to the beach in Halkidiki and floated in the sea.

"That's a great spot," he said, brightening.

***

A month or so later, I came across a scribbled phone number. I had met Fotini inside the dining hall at the Greek church in Oakland where we both came to help set up the annual cultural festival. Tall and in her mid-sixties, she had been busily unfolding metal chairs when I introduced myself, saying my tutor had suggested I contact her. I told her I had lived in Greece and that my father had been in the CIA. I said I was working on a writing project about the coup.

"My father was in the junta," she had said to me. "Call when you get back, and I'll show you photographs." She wrote her number on a narrow slip of paper.

I grabbed my phone and dialed her number. Fotini picked up after a few rings and said she was free the following weekend.

"Come and we can talk about fathers," she said.

That Saturday, I drove three hours and arrived in California's Central Valley. MapQuest led me to a small street abutting a golf course. I parked, walked up to the house, and knocked. Fotini greeted me with a kind smile and ushered me inside.

"First, let me show you the garden," she said.

We walked out into the small, sunny backyard. It was a modest plot, no more than ten feet square, but it was ordered and growing.

"When I moved here a year ago, there was debris everywhere. You know what they say: Give a Greek a tiny patch of earth, and they'll have something growing on every inch."

"It's beautiful," I said.

She pointed to a grape vine, green and trailing up the tall wooden fence. "I found that under a pile of trash. Now, it's healthy and has almost reached the top!"

I marveled at how neat and thriving everything was. Her bean plants were full and her leafy cherry tomato hid dozens of small red globes.

When we stepped back inside, Fotini invited me to take a chair but chose the floor for herself, leaning back against the futon sofa. She asked about my trip, and I shrugged. "I found some things but not everything. I still don't really know what my dad did there. I didn't get access to the terrace at Bouboulinas Street."

"Your trip was perfect," she said, and explained that for Greeks, "perfect" didn't mean some type of ideal like it did in English. It simply meant complete. Done. Accomplished. "If on the last day of your life, if all you did was take a good shit, it was still a perfect life. Complete."

We both laughed.

"That makes me feel better," I said, smiling.

That afternoon, I asked her about her father and his roots. She described a man from the village, uneducated. She said they had a difficult relationship. She talked about being a teenager during the military junta. Other teenagers made fun of her for being the daughter of a military official, so she'd relied on Greek mythology to give her a way to understand herself and her father.

"He was a part of the junta, and he was an old-fashioned father figure. You had them everywhere in Greece in those days. He took care of many people from his home village. He was always doing favors. This was part of his sense of honor. If he knew you or your family, he helped you. It didn't matter whether you were a rightist or a leftist. You were his family. This is who he was."

Fotini got up and went over to the bookshelf. She pulled out a photo album and showed me photographs of her father. I peered at a small image of a man with a stoic face.

"He died a few years ago," Fotini said. "He went through a lot. He achieved a lot in his career. He was a serious man." She paused for a moment. "He was many things."

I felt the weight of Fotini's struggle to understand her father. She had been open with me, and I didn't want to add to her burden. Still, I had to ask.

"Do you think your dad participated in any of the torture?"

"I don't think my father did those things. Can I see him inside an interrogation room? Okay, I can. Maybe a quick punch to the gut, a kick to the balls. Yes, I can see that. But to plan to do torture over and over. I cannot see this."

I nodded and thanked Fotini for talking to me. We hugged and said goodbye.

On the drive home, I thought about the way the jagged parts of Fotini's father sat side by side inside her—the poverty and simplicity of his childhood, the way he rose through the ranks of the military. She seemed to know and accept him not just as a father but as a person. A difficult acceptance but a true one. I felt hopeful as I made my way back to Oakland. Maybe something like this was possible for me and Dad. Maybe.

30. Spy Family Closet

Not long after, I stood in the kitchen, scooping dry cat food into bowls, when Dad called.

"I'm writing a book," he said.

I lowered the bowls in slow motion to the floor. He said it was about his first assignment working on the Cuban Missile Crisis, and that the U.S. Army War College had planned to publish it. He was being the father I didn't recognize again—divulging information about his career, mostly to other people.

"Great!" I said. I hoped he heard the acceptance and interest in my voice.

"I'll send it to you when it comes out," he said.

I told him I looked forward to reading it.

When we hung up, I stared at the cat bowls. Dad had reached out to me. He was writing about an aspect of his career. It took the announcement of him writing a book for the full weight of sadness to hit me. All the years we had lost. He was 74 years old. I was grateful for the connection we were developing, but it underscored the fact that we hadn't been in each other's daily lives in decades. We couldn't get that time back—the time lost to our estrangement. To his career. To our differences.

But he was trying, telling me about his book while I still hadn't told him much about mine. All it would have taken was a few words. But how could I tell him my book was about the junta but also about *him*? I reasoned he must know this already. We had

had conversations. I had asked about his childhood and why he'd joined the agency. He knew I was researching the junta. It couldn't have been a huge stretch to think that he might be part of my book. But the simple truth was that I didn't have the courage to actually tell him. He wasn't just a part of the book; he was the focus of it.

Fear was one reason I didn't say more about my book. Another was that, after having written hundreds of pages, none of it seemed to be working. I had no idea where my project was going. I no longer knew what it was about. I wasn't mad at Dad to the same extent anymore, not personally. My research wasn't leading me anywhere new either. I felt lost. The question was how to get un-lost. Was it by continuing to write? By stopping? Focusing on my relationship with Susan? I had a life—I wasn't really lost—so why did I feel like I was?

Months later, I was home with the flu, surrounded by tissues and empty tea mugs. I stared at my laptop. *There must be something in all my pages that works.* I searched for a section that made sense, one story out of everything I had written that I could turn into a successful piece of writing. Something to mark all the hours, months, and years I'd spent on this obsessive mission. I landed on the story of Mom outing Dad during the Sunday drive. The basics of the scene were there: Mom's anger at Dad's secret, his evasiveness, my joining in trying to get him to open up. In a moment of clarity and determination, I revised and revised it until it felt complete. A stand-alone piece. When it was done, I read it aloud. Panic set in. I couldn't share this publicly. It didn't matter that Dad had retired and taught courses on the CIA. He was even working on his own book. He was moving forward, out in the open about who he was. Meanwhile, I was still keeping his secret, one I wasn't supposed to tell. Ever. Dad had joined the CIA. He'd made a choice. But it wasn't a job for me or a choice. I was born into it.

I felt a deep sense of being judged, as if Dad and Evelyn were in the room with me, along with my uncle Tom and my cousins.

Everyone shaking their heads ominously. *This will ruin you,* their expressions said. *It will ruin us.* Only Mom was there encouraging me, along with a small internal voice that said *telling is good.*

I sent a query to the Op-ed editor at the *Los Angeles Times,* pitching it as an essay about outing spies. It was in the news then. CIA agent Valerie Plame had been outed in 2003 by a columnist who said her identity was leaked by someone in President George W. Bush's administration, namely Vice President Dick Cheney's Chief of Staff, Scooter Libby. Libby was convicted of perjury and obstruction of justice in connection to the leak. And now, President Bush was deciding whether or not to pardon Libby. I pressed "send." I told myself not to expect a response. *At least you tried.*

The next morning, there was an email from the *Times* accepting the essay.

Susan congratulated me. I wanted to be happy too, but there were a hundred alarms inside me, and they were all going off. I felt like I couldn't breathe.

I made an emergency appointment with my therapist. I sat across from her and sobbed. I shouldn't have done this. She told me I was doing nothing wrong. She said that I'd fallen into a kind of family cave. She said this feeling was connected to the past, not the present. She told me that I was not disrespecting my family. She said all the right things. I couldn't take in her words. I was a child who had broken the spy family code of silence. *A bad, bad daughter.*

For the next two weeks, the editor and I emailed back and forth. We made small changes to the piece. I fought to remember that I had a right to my story. I reached out to friends for support. They told me it would be okay. Their words sounded wrong, like they didn't apply to me. I asked Susan over and over again if what I was doing was good. Did it make me a bad daughter? I asked more than I should have. I started to think she would worry that I was a fraud and not the smart and strong woman she fell in love with.

Every day that passed, the publication date drew closer. I argued with myself about telling Dad. I pictured his fury when he read it. We'd come so far—maybe not all the way, but closer. Could a 1,200-word story erase all of that?

"You need to show it to him," Susan said at breakfast, days before it was scheduled to run.

I wrote an email. My sentences were short. I couldn't think of how to lessen the effects of what I had to say: "I wrote about how I found out you were in the CIA. An editor at the *LA Times* wants to publish it. Let me know if there's anything you want to change."

For the rest of the day, I sank into anxiety as I checked my email compulsively.

The next morning, I found a voicemail from Dad telling me to give him a call. I played the message over and over, trying to gauge his emotions. Was he angry? Distracted?

When I called back, he said, "There are some things about my career you need to correct in your article." Surprisingly, he didn't sound upset, and I reasoned that maybe things would be okay. "I can tell you the correct information later, dates and names of things mostly."

My breath stilled.

"But the rest is your story to tell."

I exhaled. He had just given me permission to publish it. It felt like he had given me a kind of blessing too. A light happiness came over me.

The next morning, I stood in the kitchen making coffee when I noticed another voicemail, this one from Cindy. "You've just signed our death certificates," she said before abruptly hanging up.

I played the message for Susan.

She shook her head. "You haven't done anything. She's overreacting. She's not in any danger." Susan was reasonable, logical.

A few hours later, the phone rang, but I let it go to voicemail.

It was Dad. He left a new message, his tone ominous. "We need to talk. I'll call you later."

I waited for his call but received a fax of my essay instead. Words were circled and crossed out, and notes had been scribbled in the margins. I tried to block out my feelings to read what he'd written, the actual words, but I couldn't. *I've put everyone in danger* was all I could think. The words went round and round in my head.

When I finally reached Dad, he didn't sound the way he had yesterday. His voice was tight, his words clipped. "Are you mad at me about something here? What's your motivation for writing this?"

"I'm not mad," I said. But was that true? Hadn't I been mad at him my whole life? My breath shortened. I couldn't sort it all out. "These are things I'm trying to work out. This is what it was like for me when I found out you were in the CIA. It's my story." But it didn't feel like my story. Not really. It still felt like I was telling *his* story, something I was never supposed to do.

He directed my attention to the second paragraph. I looked down at the fax.

"You say that when I mention I was once in the CIA, it's as if I'm blowing my own cover. I've never blown my cover. Everything I say is vetted by the agency. There's no blowing any cover. I want you to change that."

His voice was a staccato in my ear as he gave orders. I started to pace the kitchen. I tried to focus on what he was saying. He wasn't talking about my part of the story; he was talking about his part. I tried to stay present, push away my panic. He hated this phrase, "blowing his cover." He merely wanted that to be taken out.

"It's just a way of talking," I said.

"It's not accurate. That should come out of the piece."

My legs wobbled. "Okay, I'll think about it."

"Let's switch to something else," he said. "You say here that the CIA runs drugs. That hurts. It really does."

"I didn't mean you ran drugs. I meant others. The CIA in general."

My breath seized. I felt like I was losing my ability to process, to speak.

I said, "I'm just trying to describe my beliefs. What about the crack epidemic in the eighties? The CIA was implicated in that. I'm not saying you are." I could tell I was making things worse. "Maybe I can take that part out."

I felt myself giving up, agreeing to everything he wanted. He didn't say anything about how it had felt for me to be told cover stories as a kid. The fact that it might have made it harder for me to trust him, which in turn may have contributed to the barriers between us. Obstacles that were still there, even in this very call. He glossed over all of that as if I hadn't written it. He gave me the dates of his service in Vietnam and Grenada. I scribbled down the information.

After the call, I was exhausted. I stood in the kitchen, breathing hard. He had seemed okay with it at first. Then something changed. What had happened between his first and second phone call to me? I was a zombie for the rest of the day. I walked and moved, but I couldn't feel anything.

Evelyn called. I didn't know who had told her—Dad or Cindy.

"Don't print it," she said. "Dad's old now."

Her words were like knives. Evelyn used to be my ally when it came to Dad. But now she was on his side. I wanted to take back what I had done. Erase it all.

I drove up to the spiritual center for a session with someone I trusted. I needed support beyond Susan and my friends. I met with a woman who had kind eyes. She invited me to see the opportunity in this situation. She said, "Truths are coming out. This is so positive!"

I felt a glow from her voice and heart, but the minute I left her office, it was gone.

You can stop this from happening, I told myself. *There is still time. You can pull the piece.* But there was another voice. *Maybe it will be okay,* it whispered.

Dad called the day before the article was scheduled to run and left a message. He wanted an update, but I couldn't face him anymore. I didn't return it. I took a sleeping pill that night. In the morning, the horizon slanted, and my feet moved unsteadily beneath me. I went to my Saturday yoga class. Afterward, I found Susan waiting for me, a giant smile on her face.

"It's out online."

I smiled weakly. We drove to a newsstand and bought a copy of the paper. There it was. The story that had lived inside me for so long was finally out in the open.

When we got home, I found dozens of messages in my inbox, many from other spy kids. Strangers. There was a breathless quality, as if there wasn't enough time to say what needed saying.

"Me too. My dad was a spy," they said.

One man wrote, "The secret we carry is bigger than us."

He told me he felt responsible for keeping his father's secret and said he could never do what I did. His dad could be killed if his identity were revealed. He warned me not to use his name in anything I wrote. He seemed disapproving of my piece but then added, "It's good to see my life on the page."

Another man sent a recording of the theme song from *The Spy Who Loved Me.*

He said he played it often and that listening to it allowed him to feel connected to his father. He said his father never opened up to him about his work. I pressed play and listened to the sweeping arrangement, a song I used to make fun of. Today, it sounded like a sweet, loving tribute. But it saddened me too, to think that there was no other public way for him to honor his father and their connection except a theme song from a film franchise that glorified spydom. But I understood. Spy families were invisible. Intentionally so.

Daughters wrote me too.

"I used to tell people what my father did, but people reacted with argument or stony silence. I don't tell anyone anymore." I understood this all too well—the way saying the word "CIA" stopped conversations.

Another woman said she put it together that her father had been in the CIA while she was watching a movie about Vietnam. "That's when it clicked," she wrote. She said her father had never confirmed he had worked for the CIA. She thanked me for my piece, for "putting it out there."

One woman told me a different family secret. She described the sexual abuse she experienced in her family and said she had never told anyone this before. "You are the first person I've ever told."

I wrote back and told her that she was brave. I encouraged her to find more people in her life who were safe to tell.

I went through each email, one by one, and responded.

I got to the last email and saw a single line: "Is your dad Mike Absher?"

Shit. Someone knows Dad.

I immediately tried to distance myself from whoever this was. I said I couldn't give any more information. I had only intended for strangers to read it, not people who actually knew Dad. The next day, the same person emailed again.

"I definitely know your father! We were in Vietnam at the same time. I went to his office at the Bush School and showed your dad the article!"

My stomach dropped. He showed it to Dad? The exclamation marks confused me. Was this man saying he liked my piece and thought Dad did too? I tried to picture Dad in his office. He held the newspaper in his hand. He saw the graphic image the *Times* included—a floating set of horn-rimmed glasses, just like the ones he wore when I was little. I was tempted to write back and ask if he thought Dad had approved of the piece, but I held back.

Cindy left another upsetting voicemail. Susan said to tune her out, but Cindy's words spun inside my mind anyway—*I can't believe you would do this to your father.*

Dad called while I was working with a student the following week. His message sounded cheery, as if the rupture in our relationship caused by *the article* had never happened.

"I sure am proud..." he started and then stalled.

I stood in the kitchen, gripping the phone, anticipating what he was about to say.

"...of your work with students," he said, finishing.

Had he been about to say he was proud of the article but then stopped himself?

Days that felt like weeks passed with no phone calls between us.

On my birthday, Susan made my favorite cake, a Betty Crocker mix from the box, the way Mom used to make it. Friends came over. The house was loud and full, so when the phone rang I missed it. I went into another room and played the message from Dad.

In it, he sang the "Happy Birthday" song, the way he did every birthday since I was a kid. He sang it loud and full and all the way through. My chest heaved as I listened to his final intonation... "Happy birthday, dear Leslie... happy birthday to you!" I played it back again and again. Each time, I felt my love for him and his for me. It was a simple thing, but it felt immutable.

31. Tailing a Spy

The roar of telling my story in the *LA Times* receded. I still felt like a bad daughter for publishing it—every time I thought of what I had done my breath caught—but the worst was over. A wide quiet settled between Dad and me. It was in the midst of this lull that Dad sent an email saying his book about the Cuban Missile Crisis had come out.

"I'm very interested in hearing your comments!" he wrote.

I couldn't believe he wanted my opinion after everything that had happened with the *LA Times* story. But what exactly had happened? I didn't fully know. The experience had deeply unsettled me, whereas Dad seemed to have moved on. Had Cindy and my sister? I had no idea.

A week later, Dad's book *Mindsets and Missiles: A Firsthand Account of the Cuban Missile Crisis* arrived. I started it immediately. It was an academic account but surprisingly open. And critical. Dad felt the United States hadn't had enough early intelligence on the existence of missiles in Cuba because the Kennedy administration had been too cautious to approve reconnaissance flights. "When our national security is at stake, we should not hesitate to undertake risky intelligence collection operations including espionage, to penetrate our adversary's deceptions." It read like a manifesto for taking calculated risks.

But it was a passage about the days leading up to the reconnaissance flights that grabbed my attention. Dad wrote that he had received three crucial reports that built the case for the flights. The first was from an agent in Cuba who reported a conversation with Fidel Castro's personal pilot. The pilot is quoted as telling the agent, "We have 40-mile range guided missiles, both surface-to-surface and surface-to-air, and we have a radar system which covers, sector by sector, all of the Cuban air space and (beyond) as far as Florida...They don't know what is awaiting them." The pilot was in a privileged position to overhear Castro's confidential conversations, and the agent was reliable.

The second report was an eyewitness account of a Soviet missile seen in transport. The eyewitness described and drew an image of the weapon in great detail. More evidence that missiles were on the island.

But the third report was perhaps the most important.

In it, an agent gave coordinates for a large geographic zone in the Pinar del Rio Province, where "very secret and important work is in progress, believed to be concerned with missiles." Another witness corroborated this, spotting "Soviet flat-bed trailers carrying large tubes extending over the end of the trailers, heading toward Pinar del Rio..." Dad wrote that he'd passed on these reports immediately, as they came in, and that while each contributed to making the case for flights, it was the report of the geographic zone "that became the photographic target of the U-2 flight on October 14 that first photographed the Soviet SS-4 missiles."

I was riveted. Dad had been at the epicenter of the unfolding crisis. He had played a key role in it by reviewing and passing on crucial intelligence. I saw him in a new light. He had diligently reviewed and passed on intel that had led to a de-escalation of tensions between the U.S. and the Soviet Union, ultimately preventing war. I knew Dad would see his work as part of a team, and that others contributed to this positive outcome as much as he did. That's how he always talked. I saw this too, but I also saw *him*. My father. An individual doing critical work at a crucial moment in history.

When I finished, I sent him an email. I said I had found it to be a fascinating insider account. And that he had done such important work. Just as I hoped he saw me in my article, I wanted him to know that I was at least trying to see him in what he wrote. I didn't mention my own writing, but I sensed it in the background, sensed the interplay between our words. A shared impulse to break old silences.

***

That summer, Susan and I traveled to Texas for a cousin's wedding. I sent Dad and Cindy an email saying we'd love to see them. I didn't get my hopes up. My last visit with Dad, the one shortly before our commitment ceremony five years earlier, was a disaster and one I didn't want to repeat. I told myself that the connection we had now was good enough. We were back in each other's lives. We were talking. Even after the *LA Times* essay.

Dad emailed back saying, "Let's get together."

I was stunned and excited.

Susan and I flew to Texas. After the wedding in San Antonio, we made our plans to head north to the small town of Bryan. Dad and I had already gone over the directions to his house, but he insisted on meeting us halfway and guiding us.

I told him we had GPS and that he didn't have to do that.

"There's a big game in town," he said. "It's gonna be a zoo."

On the day of our visit, like a page out of a John le Carré novel, Susan and I approached the agreed-upon highway exit and pulled onto the shoulder behind Dad's midsized American car. He gave a quick wave and led us off the shoulder. We followed behind for a few short miles and turned into a Marriott where he had arranged a room for Susan and me. We parked, and I watched Dad get out of his car—cane first, then one leg, then the other, and finally a giant push to standing. I left the car and walked toward him. At 75, he was still commanding, the way he had been during my childhood, but he walked with a stoop now. He seemed frailer than our visit five years before.

We both smiled big and came together for a hug. I marveled at the miracle of this moment. Everything felt easy. But as we hugged, the force of my body caused him to tip backward slightly, and I realized he was old, fragile. He regained his balance but not with the same strength he used to have. Tears welled up and I looked away, which caused me to catch only the tail end of the hug he gave to Susan.

The three of us made our way inside. Dad used his cane to shuffle up to the front desk.

"I've already paid for this with points," he said to the concierge who couldn't find his name in the computer. Uh-oh. He was getting impatient. My neck tensed.

A moment later, the woman said she had found his name. She gave Susan and me a card key each and smiled. Dad said he'd wait for us in the car and turned to make his way back outside. Susan and I wheeled our bags down the hallway.

"I can't believe how well things are going," I said.

We clicked into our room and stepped into a spacious, light-filled suite.

Susan stopped abruptly. "Wow," she said.

I followed her eyes to the middle of the room and saw a king-size bed. Not two beds. One. I stared at the bed and what it meant. I had started my coming-out process years ago and had even come out to Dad in my 20s in a letter. But it hadn't stuck. I rushed back into the closet and withheld my life from him for years. I didn't tell him about my breakups, or how lonely I felt, or any aspect of my struggle to accept my sexuality. It took therapy, Pride parades, books, queer friends, and gradually my own courage. Dad hadn't witnessed any of this. It was as if my sexuality had stayed locked in silence between us. Until now. I stared at the wide bed with its floral covering. I felt fully out to him for the first time. And fully accepted.

Back outside, Susan and I got into the rental car and followed Dad out of the retail area. A minute later, he called to see if we wanted to stop by the George Bush School of Government and Public Service where he taught at Texas A & M to see where he worked. I knew he was a Fellow at the Scowcroft Institute of International Affairs, but I didn't know much else.

"Sure!" I said.

The parking lot was empty when we arrived. Susan pulled into a spot, and Dad slid into one next to ours. His passenger window lowered smoothly.

"That's where I teach," he half yelled, pointing to a gray building. His blue eyes were hidden in the shadow of his Dallas Cowboys cap, but I could tell he was excited. In the middle of the courtyard between these buildings, I spotted a sculpture.

I pointed and asked him what it was.

"That's a real piece of the Berlin Wall!" he said enthusiastically, sounding like a kid.

I told him I wanted to take a picture of it, hoping he saw how I wanted to honor his life and career.

"Great!" he said and sent his window up to wait.

Susan and I got out of the car and made our way over to the sculpture, a handful of bronze Mustangs in mid-leap over a piece of graffiti-covered concrete. They were fierce and beautiful, nostrils flared and eyes blazing. They seemed ready to escape from the platform and run forever under the wide Texas sky. Beneath the sculpture, a plaque read, "The Day the Wall Came Down." The symbolism was unmistakable. Freedom had overleapt the rubble of communism.

After I took photographs, Dad led us to their house. Cindy was there. I expected her disapproval, but she greeted us warmly. Dad took us into his study. He pointed out framed political and historical memorabilia he had collected over the course of his career, including an autographed photo of President George H.W. Bush. I nodded, hoping Dad saw that I was okay with his politics and with who he was.

Cindy gave Susan and me a tour of the rest of the house. We chatted comfortably about the art she had collected from Dad's different postings. Mom's paintings were also prominently displayed throughout the house, reflecting Cindy's care and attention to that part of Dad's life and mine. When we circled back to the kitchen, Cindy and Susan fell into a conversation about vintage cookbooks.

Afterward, we sat down to lunch.

I looked over at Susan, happy for this small and ordinary moment. We chatted about the weather and cats, but this time it didn't feel like small talk. It just felt good.

32. Soldier

Susan and I returned to Oakland, and Dad and I returned to our pre-*LA Times* bimonthly phone calls. Just as we returned to our rhythm and I started to enjoy a new kind of normal between us, Cindy called to say that he had fallen on his way to his office at the Bush School.

"I had to urge him to go to the emergency room," she said. "There's bleeding inside his skull. They have to operate immediately."

Evelyn and I flew to Texas to help.

When we arrived at his hospital room, Dad was weak and his speech slurred. Cindy looked exhausted. She had spent all morning communicating with his doctors and trying to correct problems with his care. Evelyn and I stood beside his bed. We talked to Dad and told him we were there, without making eye contact with each other. At lunch, in the hospital's sunny courtyard, we sat at separate tables. I called Susan to give her the update and watched Evelyn eat her salad, her long gray hair hanging gracefully around her face.

After lunch, we helped Cindy by wheeling Dad to his speech therapy appointment. Inside the room, the five of us sat around a small round table and a bookshelf—Dad, Cindy, me, Evelyn, and the therapist. Dad sat in his wheelchair, staring straight ahead. He seemed angry. At us? At his predicament? He seemed reluctant to do the exercises and said he knew how to read "just fine." The therapist was patient. Gradually, she walked him through the exercises designed to help him regain his speech. At one point, he seemed on the verge of an impatient outburst. I cringed. I looked over at Evelyn to see if she felt the same way, but she wouldn't meet my gaze.

After a week, Dad's speech and strength improved. I returned to Oakland.

A few days later, I drove to the public pool where I had swum ever since moving to California. Instead of grabbing my bag and heading down to the locker room, I looked out at the hundred-year-old oak tree growing on the dry hillside above the pool. Dad would be turning seventy-seven that year. I pulled out my cellphone and dialed.

When he answered, his voice had its usual resonance.

I wanted to tell him that I would miss him. That I knew he wouldn't always be around. I wanted to say all the things I still hadn't—about my journey for answers and my need to tell my truth. About the sadness of all the years we hadn't opened up to each other. Instead, I asked about his recovery.

"I hate physical therapy, but it's helping," he said.

He told me he was working on another book.

"That's great!" I said.

He described the topic—a review of all the Presidential Intelligence Advisory Boards since the first one began in 1956. I said I had never even heard of Presidential Advisory Boards. He said most people hadn't. He described panels comprised of nonpartisan experts tasked with advising presidents about intelligence collection, analysis and estimates, and the legality of operations abroad. He hadn't been on one of these boards and said he was co-authoring it with two others—a university professor and a foreign service professional. He asked how my day was going. I said I was at my local pool, sitting in my car about to go for a swim.

"Swimming before work—what a great schedule!" He seemed genuinely happy for me.

I remembered growing up, the young and more relaxed Dad of my early childhood, and how we rode the waves together—in the Mediterranean and the Gulf Coast. Me riding on his back while he shielded me from the waves.

After we said goodbye, I got out of the car and descended the steps to the recreational building. I held onto our easy exchange as I changed into my suit. A moment later, I moved into the water, my arms pulling me to the end and back again. This was us now. New. Different.

***

Not long after, Dad was in the hospital again. He called from the ICU.

Susan and I had been at her mother's birthday celebration in Washington State. A table with an enormous green cake sat in the middle of the room. Her brothers, sisters-in-law, and niece and nephews were there. My phone rang, and I ducked into the bedroom to talk.

"I have pancreatic cancer," Dad said in his characteristic plain-speak way.

I froze.

"It doesn't look like I have much time left." The regret in his voice was clear.

Sadness swept through me. Susan and I left that afternoon and flew to Texas.

When we arrived at the hospital, Cindy was there, and so was Evelyn.

Dad lay under his hospital bed sheet, his eyes closed. It hurt to see him so fragile and pale.

My eyes filled with tears. "I'm here, Dad."

Cindy gave us the update. "The doctors say it's inoperable. They said it's in a bad position." She looked devastated, and I saw how helpless she must have felt. And how fatigued. She turned to Dad and said, "Look what I have, Honey." She rummaged around in her bag and lifted out the galley of Dad's new book, propping it in front of him so he could see it: *Privileged and Confidential: The Secret History of the President's Intelligence Advisory Board.* There were three authors, and Dad's name was the first. Dad immediately popped his eyes open to take in the book and its cover. His glasses sat slightly askew, but he was able to read the title. We all congratulated Dad and smiled through our tears.

Everything happened fast after that. Cindy struggled to let me and Evelyn help her make decisions. When the doctors told us we had to start thinking about letting him go, she talked about cutting-edge procedures available in Houston. I wanted this to be true, but when I pulled his doctor aside in the hallway, she said little could be done. I tried to focus on being with Dad in the moments I could after that. My old disappointments vanished. I felt like I was just starting to learn who he was. His apology had caused my resentments to fade, but it was his books too, and our phone calls—more honest and less guarded than they used to be—that made a difference. That afternoon, I reached for Dad's hand and held it. *Just be here,* I told myself. It felt like a miracle to no longer feel conflicted about us. To feel sad but also present.

The next day, a couple arrived from Dad's church. They slipped into the hospital room where Susan, me, Cindy, and Evelyn stood, watching Dad. They told me what a good man he was. They held rosaries and bibles. Their faces were kind. I introduced Susan as my partner, and they shook her hand.

"Do you want to join us in a prayer?" they asked.

We nodded and joined hands with them. Their warm energy comforted me inside the room with all its ticking machines. They began reciting the prayers I had grown up with. "Our Father in heaven, hallowed be thy name . . ." Dad's eyes were closed, but we knew he heard us. After this, Cindy asked Susan to say a prayer, and she did. It was a different kind of prayer, an affirmation that wasn't at all Catholic, but no one minded. Something felt complete inside me. I was meant to be here right now. It had all been for this.

In the evening, another friend from Dad and Cindy's church visited the hospital—a small woman with lively eyes. "I want you to know I'm here for you," she said. She embraced me and Susan and squeezed both our hands. She said that growing up with a dad in the agency couldn't have been easy. I told her it wasn't, grateful for her compassion. It was a small acknowledgment, just a few words, but it amazed me.

For the next few days, I spent my time in small conversations. I told Dad I loved him and that everything was okay between us. There were no more bridges to cross. We had arrived at a kind of peace. Gratitude flooded me. But so did regret. I was no longer angry, but I didn't really know him. We hadn't had the time to form a new relationship. If we had been sitting around a restaurant table, and he had been well, what would we have talked about? I didn't know. I sat beside him not saying anything. I realized I didn't know how to talk to him. I stared out his window at the shiny grackles perched on a telephone wire.

That night we decided—Susan, Evelyn, and me—to go to a German restaurant outside the city. We ordered sweet white wine and drank it quietly. Evelyn, who normally never drank, had a glass too. After a few minutes, she spoke up.

"I'm sorry I pulled away after you sold your Boston house," she said.

I felt a rush of relief. "I'm sorry too," I said back.

It didn't seem important to rehash everything. All the conversations we'd had—me moving thousands of miles away, her shutting me out—none of that mattered. We didn't need to take sides anymore.

We ate the rest of our meal talking about Dad, our jobs, our lives.

***

The next day, Susan flew back to California for a work obligation. It was just me, Evelyn, and Cindy at the hospital. Cindy said she wanted a second opinion. Evelyn and I conferred again with his primary doctor.

"I wish I had better news," she said.

Cindy contacted another doctor and dismissed his primary. I could tell she was hurting, but so was I. Through it all, Dad had been one of my life's anchors. His presence intermittent yet steady. There was so much left for us to say. But if I stayed, I realized Dad's last days would be filled with tension, something I didn't want. I decided to leave. I entered his room and whispered that I loved him. I felt full with our healing and knew that it didn't matter where I was—we would always be connected. I didn't want to go, but knowing that Evelyn would stay comforted me.

Evelyn and I took the elevator to the lobby and walked to my car.

"I'll call you with how it's going," she said.

I told her she could call just to talk too.

We hugged, and I got into the rental car and drove to the airport.

When Dad was released to palliative care at home, Evelyn called with the update. I felt like we were sisters again. She said she had visited Dad in the morning and that he wasn't in any pain. I thanked her for being there. She said she was doing it for both of us.

The next day, she called and asked if I wanted to talk to Dad. She said he couldn't speak but he listened and understood what everyone was saying. She put the receiver to his ear.

"Hi, Dad," I said. How many times had I said those words? Our connection over the course of my life had existed primarily over the phone. Our conversations had always preceded with these words—whether we were working things out, making small talk, or in conflict. Our voices across phone wires had carried us along. And it carried us still.

"I just want you to know that I love you," I said.

My face streamed with tears.

I needed to say more. I reached for a way to signal to him that if he worried about our relationship, he needn't. "Everything is good between us, Dad," I said. It felt awkward to utter this. We had said "I love you" throughout my life but had almost never explicitly talked about our relationship. Could such a big idea be encapsulated like that, the distance shrunk with just these words? I hoped so.

***

I was at an art school open house with Susan and her nephew when Evelyn rang. I stepped into the parking lot and heard my sister's voice.

"He's gone," she said. She said he'd died peacefully in his room.

Susan and her nephew came out and found me leaning against the brick building staring at nothing. They embraced me.

A deafening silence overtook everything for weeks and months after he died. I talked to Susan, Evelyn, and Cindy, but they seemed miles away. Sometimes my phone rang, and I hardly noticed. I rode along the bike path and watched yellow leaves turn inside a rushing wind, but I didn't hear the wind's voice. The sound I wanted to hear most was absent.

***

Uncle Tom and his wife, Erika, came for the memorial service. My cousin, Matthew, was there too, along with Evelyn, Susan, and Mom's sister, Aunt Anne, and her brother, my Uncle Phil. On the day of the service, the church slowly filled. Hundreds of people arrived. Andrew Card, President George W. Bush's Chief of Staff—now the Acting Dean of the Bush School of Government and Public Service where Dad had taught—rose from his pew. He cited Dad's more than 31 years with the CIA in the National Clandestine

Service; his teaching positions at the University of Texas at San Antonio and the National Defense Intelligence College; his work on the Joint Terrorism Task Force in San Antonio; and the accountability review boards he served under appointment from Secretary of State Condoleezza Rice to investigate terrorist attacks in Iraq. He spoke of Dad's many accomplishments with the agency—Chief of Station in two countries, Chief of Base in two others, and numerous awards and citations, including twice being awarded the Intelligence Medal of Merit. I realized the magnitude of Dad's career and accomplishments. For the first time, I felt the importance and impact of his work. The full stature of it.

Tom stepped up to the podium.

His voice cracked as he began the eulogy. He described a day when he and Dad, not yet teenagers, were sent by train to a summer camp in Michigan to avoid the polio outbreak sweeping Texas. They had boarded their train, and when they did, they saw that it was full of young GIs headed overseas.

"Some were just a handful of years older than we were," Tom said.

He speculated that this might have been a turning point for Dad. He said they watched these soldiers in awe, as heroes going off to fight the Nazis, but, he said, "My brother watched them especially closely. He took in their demeanor, as if he were preparing himself for his own future without knowing it.

"Later, when my brother joined the CIA, it was as if an invisible door had closed. Michael was on one side of the door, and the rest of us were on the other. My brother had slipped away from us. From then on, there were things he couldn't share. I see it now as a kind of sacrifice but also a kind of loss. For all of us. Especially my brother."

Tom returned to his pew, and I saw the emotion brimming in his eyes.

After the service, the reception room filled with people from Dad's life—members of his prayer circle, colleagues from the Joint FBI Task Force, the academics who had co-authored his second book, and current and former students from the Bush School of Government. One of his students, a woman in a navy blue skirt, approached me. She told me how much she had learned from Dad and how engaging he was as a teacher. She described the way he had been a mentor to her.

"He loved to tell stories from the field," she said.

She said he was warm and that he laughed a lot. I listened to her describe a side of the dad I remembered and the one I had never gotten the chance to know. She knew him. So did a lot of the people in the room. They talked about having had a relationship with a person that I didn't, not in the way they had. I had searched for answers about his career and assignments in order to understand him, but the people in this room actually knew him. *They* had the answers.

***

The burial was weeks later in Dad's hometown of San Antonio. Instead of being buried in the same cemetery as Mom, his wishes were to be buried at a military cemetery. Unlike his memorial, Dad's burial felt intimate, attended by close friends and family. We all stood beneath an awning across the path from Dad's burial site. The weather was warm. A priest spoke, and just like at Mom's funeral thirty years earlier, I couldn't focus on his words. When he finished, we stood in silence and witnessed a 21-gun salute, each shot piercing the air. Then a soldier in formal dress stepped forward. He removed the American flag that covered Dad's casket and began the process of folding it—slowly and ceremoniously. He turned each corner methodically until the flag was assembled into the shape of a triangle. White stars showed against a background of deep blue. The soldier stepped toward Cindy and, with both hands, presented the flag to her.

Afterward, everyone left for a nearby chapel, except for Evelyn and me and one of our cousins. The three of us stayed behind and watched the cemetery workers ready the ground. They placed Dad's casket onto a transporter and moved it to the gravesite. Then they placed his casket inside a container, pressed a lever, and slowly lowered him into the ground. I didn't think it would affect me so much to see his body placed into the earth, but it did.

33. Condolence Card

A year after Dad died, Cindy sent me a box containing Dad's high school yearbook, some of his magic tricks, and an envelope of cards and letters. Inside the envelope, I found condolence notes from when Mom had died over thirty years before. Many were from her San Antonio friends, whose names I didn't recognize. The cards were white or pastel blue with misty messages about death and loss. There was one card with the words *In Sympathy* embossed in gold on the front. Inside, it held a preprinted message, and below this a name, the card signer's only addition—*Gust Avrakotos*.

I stared at the name of the rogue CIA officer who had run the underground station in Athens, the spy featured in *Charlie Wilson's War*, someone Dad pretended not to know when I had asked. But that had been another deception. He *had* known Gust Avrakotos. They were friends, close enough for Gust to send Dad a sympathy card. I stared at the signature. Dad was gone. I had stopped investigating the junta. But seeing Gust's signature had opened something up inside me again.

I talked with Susan over breakfast. "I don't want to do this."

"What about your questions?" she asked, irritated.

"I just can't." I wanted her to tell me it was time to stop, that I had done enough.

She just stared at me.

Later, I realized she was right. I had tried to convince myself that I was through, but I wasn't. Not really. The coup and Dad's role still haunted me—answers or no answers.

I began working on another essay, one about my conflicted feelings—my love for Dad and for Greece. In it, I said I would probably never know what my father had done during the coup, and that I had to find a way to be at peace with not knowing. I spent hours revising and shaping it before sending it to a Greek news site. They accepted it and published it a few days later. Shortly after it came out, I was sitting in the living room looking through email when a Facebook message from someone named John popped up.

"I just read your essay and liked it. I knew your dad well. We worked together. He was one of the most pro-Greek officers I've ever met. Send me your email, and we can communicate privately."

My breath cut out. In all the time I had spent researching the junta and investigating Dad, I was never able to reach one of his colleagues or even a friend. I had tried once, had called the man who was his boss in Greece, but he was aging and after saying hello, he passed the phone to his wife.

I sent a reply to John and waited.

The next day, there was an email from him.

"I met your dad when I joined the CIA and was completing the tradecraft course. Your father was a class act and one of the officers who truly loved the country. He had a keen sense of the Greek people."

It lifted my spirits to read that Dad loved Greece. I had always known this but reading the words from a friend and colleague made it more real.

But it was what John wrote next that stopped me:

"I sense your consternation over the CIA's role in Greece and the colonel's regime and want to assure you that your father and the other officers serving there were not directly involved in any form of torture. We aggressively collected intelligence in response to requirements, but torture or coercion is not in our genes. Did the right-wing dictatorship practice torture? Undeniably, yes. Did we know about it? I am sure that we did. Could we have stopped it? Our mission was to report on the situation in Greece. U.S. policymakers at the time elected to support the regime, at least in the beginning, because it was anti-communist. . . Your dad was a thoughtful, sincere individual and we all trusted his judgment."

I read over John's email again after our call. *Your Dad was a thoughtful, sincere individual and we all trusted his judgment.* The simple words penetrated me. This was the father I knew to be true but for so long doubted. If I had read John's message years earlier, before investigating the coup and dictatorship, I wouldn't have believed it. I would have suspected an agenda, a bias. I was too angry then to see the gray area, the shades of truth that defined the Cold War.

Not anymore. So much had changed. I had traveled to Greece, read reports, spoken with scholars. I would never know all of it— what my father did or didn't know—but John's email had given me back the father I felt was true. And in doing so, I had finally arrived at the end of my investigation. It wasn't the end because of what John shared, although that was essential. It was the end because through John's words I gave Dad back his life. I had grown up with his secret and so had felt as if it belonged to me too, a spy daughter's legacy. But it didn't. A sense of liberation penetrated me. Dad's past belonged to him. His career. His secrets. I didn't need to carry them anymore as if they were mine. They weren't mine and never had been. I saw that now. Finally. Just as I now saw what belonged to me and only to me. This. My story to tell.

Acknowledgments

To Susan, my beloved. You never failed to find a way to help me through the fraught process of writing this story. You look into my eyes every day with love and admiration and support me ceaselessly.

To editors Jon Gosch and Kevin Breen at Latah Books. I was given a second chance by both of you and not a day goes by that I do not count myself lucky. I am grateful for your tireless championing of this book. You recognized the story I was trying to tell and rolled up your sleeves and helped me find a way to tell it. To Scott Manning and Abby Welhouse. I couldn't have had a more supportive or talented publicity team.

To my uncle, Tom. You showed me the reward of knowing myself and gave me family clues, ones you painstakingly discovered after much reflection. I couldn't have written this story or walked this road without your example and love. To Cindy Absher for your steadfast love and acceptance. To Anne Aderhold for your heart and compassion. To Linda McCarriston for being there for me when I was bereft at 16 years of age and all the years after. To Robin for your empathy and for always championing my writing. To Kit Frieden for your support. To Phil Shook, who supported and congratulated me when my first father/daughter story went out into the world (long before I was ready). To my sister, Evelyn—you walked with me through the forest of childhood and now you walk free of it all. To my cousins—you have each shared parts of this road and offered your friendship. Thank you to Jean Beneville, who told me the truth would set me free and in doing so gave me permission to write this book. To the unswerving support from Bert, Jan, Derrick, Michele, Trey, Melisa, Kaitlin, Ryan, Brandon, Blake, and Nick. My family indeed.

To Stephanie Tilton, my forever sister, and to all of my Massachusetts lesbian tribe—Jenny Coleman, Molly Froelich, Sue Grodberg, Gail Rossitter, Lynn, Efi and Daphne. You are in this book and in my heart, a part of this story in every way. From cafés to soccer pitches, Somerville to Western Mass, music festivals to backyard games. Thank you for always being there. To my swim community—intrepid explorers who understand the transcendent joys of swimming in pools or open water. To the cold waves of the San Francisco Bay for always restoring me no matter what. To Ann, who listened, and to Cindi, who reminds me to bring compassion to myself first. To all the friends far and near who supported and cheered me on.

To the writer Amalía Melis, director of Aegean Arts Circle, whose friendship nurtured me and this story from the very beginning. I am indebted to all my fellow writers at AAC, especially Diana, Jacquie, Dawn, Kristine, Lorraine, Bren, and Marylle. Each of you became a plank I could stand on. To the teachers—Natalie Bakopoulos, Robert Olen Butler, Thomas E. Kennedy, Linda Lappin, Nick Papandreou. To Dorothy Allison, who told me to write into my fear. To my amazing Bay Area writing community—Anna Edmondson, Melissa Fondakowski, Kelley Gibler, Joanne Hartman, Dianne Jacob, and Alison Luterman. And so many more. To Linden Gross, who helped me embark on this story. To Janet Goldstein, who helped bring it into readiness, and to fellow memoir writers who lit a passion in me for this kind of story——*Before Night Falls* by Reinaldo Arenas, *Another Bullshit Night in Suck City* by Nick Flynn, *Zami: A New Spelling of My Name* by Audre Lorde.

To the poets Constantine P. Cavafy, Odysseus Elytis, and George Seferis, whose Greekness I borrowed and made my own. To all of those who shared their story with me here and in

Greece. To Anna, who first taught me to speak and feel Greek. To my tutors—Tatiana, Laura, Anastasia, and Polyxeni. To Spyros Draenos for his help. To the editors at the *Greek Reporter, Los Angeles Times, Huffington Post,* and *Ms.* magazine who helped bring this story into print, piece by piece. To M.K., who reached out and brought everything full circle.

To Dad, who always knew I needed to find my own way.

And finally, to Mom, the artist Jeanette Patricia Shook, the brave one, whose prayers for me I hear every day.

About the Author

Leslie Absher is a journalist and essayist. Her work has appeared in the *Los Angeles Times, Independent, Salon, Huffington Post, Ms., Greek Reporter,* and the *San Francisco Chronicle.*

Her father joined the CIA before she was born. When she was a baby, her family moved to Athens, Greece. Just in time for a coup.

She received a master's in education from Harvard, taught G.E.D. to high school dropouts, and currently teaches writing and study skills to middle school and high school students. She lives in Oakland with her comic book writer/lawyer wife.